D1602606

BIG GAME
and
BIG GAME RIFLES

BUFFALO HULL

(Shot and photographed by C. Fletcher Jamieson, S. Rhodesia)

BIG GAME AND
BIG GAME RIFLES

by

John "Pondoro" Taylor

SAFARI PRESS, Inc.

P.O. BOX 3095, Long Beach, CA 90803, USA

Taylor, John

Safari Press, Inc.

1993, Long Beach, California

ISBN 0-940143-87-9

10 9 8 7 6 5 4 3

Readers wishing to receive the Safari Press catalog, featuring many fine books on big-game hunting, wingshooting, and sporting firearms, should write to Safari Press Inc., P.O. Box 3095, Long Beach, CA 90803, USA. Tel: (714) 894-9080 or visit our Web site at www.safaripress.com.

AUTHOR'S FOREWORD

THE following chapters were written just prior to the recent world upheaval. I amused myself during a somewhat tedious convalescence by re-writing them and adding quite considerably here and there. In general, however, there was little that required alteration.

I have said nothing about automatic or self-loading rifles, because, prior to the War, there was none of that description that could conceivably be described as a big game rifle. But one views with grave concern, the possible if not probable, if not indeed certain, introduction of full-powered weapons of that type into the realms of sport [sic] in the near future.

I have seen Bren guns and " Tommy " guns turned on game during the War. I sincerely trust that I shall never again see anything of the sort !

Automatic rifles could never be necessary for sporting purposes and would tend greatly to encourage the inexperienced and thoughtless into " browing " the herd —which would inevitably cause a vast number of wretched animals to be wounded.

One hopes that the Powers that Be with Game Preservation at heart have their eyes open to the danger and will take immediate steps to forbid the importation of such essentially unsportsmanlike weapons.

PREFACE

IT is an astonishing thing how little the average sports-man in Africa knows about the rifles he uses. It is only a trifling exaggeration to say that all that he really does know about them is: that the bullet comes out of the end that has a hole in it! And if this small book of mine can save even one young beginner, contemplating his first battery, from some of the bitter, and costly, disappointments which once were mine—through using utterly unsuitable weapons—then I shall feel that it has justified its existence.

For there can be little doubt that a book dealing with rifles suitable for all types of African hunting is badly needed. Most books on big game hunting devote a short chapter to rifles; but, in the great majority of cases, the writers of these books, having found a battery which proves satisfactory, give up experimenting and just praise and recommend those particular weapons which they are using. Consequently, a great many of these books must be read before a thorough grasp of the subject is possible; and big game hunting books are, as a rule, expensive. Major Sir Gerald Burrard, Bart., D.S.O., has filled this want in connection with Indian hunting with that splendid little volume of his *Notes on Sporting Rifles*; but, although a great deal of what holds good for one part of the big game hunting world can be applied with, perhaps, certain modifications to various other parts, nevertheless the principal type of hunting in Africa comes, as it were, midway between the two main Indian extremes: hill shooting and jungle shooting. And so it seemed to me that there might be room here in which to squeeze in this small effort of mine.

It might not, perhaps, be out of place to mention that I have been a professional elephant hunter for some

6

twenty-five years or so. And when I say twenty-five years I mean that quite literally, for I hunt from eleven and a half to twelve months a year, every year, and not just two or three months a year as is so frequently the case when men speak of " twenty-five years' big game hunting " or something of the sort. If you tot up the time that these men actually spent in the Bush, in the great majority of cases you will find that it does not amount to more than perhaps four or five years at the very most.

When I first commenced hunting, I knew nothing whatever about rifles ; never previously having used anything but a ·22-bore and a ·303 Service rifle. During the first ten years or so of my career I experimented with every conceivable make, type and bore of rifle : single, double and magazine ; good, bad and indifferent ; suitable and unsuitable ; until I discovered those which appeared to me to be definitely the best for different purposes. During the last ten years I have made few voluntary changes in my own battery, other than in barrel-length ; though I have been compelled to replace two complete batteries that were sent to the bottom of the Zambezi when, on two different occasions, hippo upset the canoe in which I was travelling. But I have still continued to use a considerable variety of weapons since, from time to time, I am asked by men with less experience to test some rifle for them and give them my opinion as to whether it is a suitable weapon or not. For my own satisfaction, and to add to my knowledge if it is one of the few bores of which I have not had personal experience— as much as to oblige the owner—naturally, I never refuse.

And it is solely in view of these facts that I venture to offer to the sporting public—but particularly to beginners —this summary of my own experiences and the conclusions to which these experiences have brought me. Of course, I fully appreciate that before it is possible to recommend any particular rifle for any particular purpose, it is most necessary to know something about the man behind the rifle : his physique and temperament cannot be entirely ignored. And, throughout the following pages, I have endeavoured to bear this fact in mind.

I am no ballistic expert. What knowledge I have of rifles has been gained solely by personally using the weapons under practical conditions of sport. It is no purpose of mine to delve deeply into the theoretical side of the question. In the first place, my knowledge of such matters is not sufficiently great ; whilst, in the second place, I rather fancy that the practical side will interest a greater number of sportsmen—particularly beginners. Accordingly, in the following pages, I have just described various incidents in my own career as a professional hunter, and in the lives of other hunters, in the hope that these incidents will serve to substantiate my arguments. In addition, I have not a little to say concerning the habits of the different species of big game ; but I consider this most necessary, because if a man knows something of the conditions under which he is liable to encounter an animal, he will be better able to appreciate why certain weapons would be more suitable for him to carry than others.

I should like to take this opportunity for expressing my very sincere thanks to Major Sir Gerald Burrard, Bart, D.S.O., for his kind and generous permission to use the ballistic and trajectory tables from that splendid little book of his, *Notes on Sporting Rifles*. But, in fairness both to Major Burrard and to myself, let me hasten to add that the right-hand column of figures, which I have headed " Knock-Out Value ", have nothing whatever to do with Major Burrard or his book. I mention this because, as a ballistic expert, it is more than probable that Major Burrard would not care to have these figures attributed to him. Nevertheless, since they approximate in such an altogether remarkable way with my own personal experience with the various rifles in actual use in the bush, I have included them in the ballistic tables as it seemed to me to be the obvious place for them.

It must be clearly understood, however, that they make no pretence of indicating " killing-power ". On the contrary, they are only to be considered as a basis for the comparison of any two rifles from the point of view of the actual knockdown blow delivered by bluff-nosed, solid, metal-covered bullets when used for head shots on heavy, massive-boned animals such as elephant. It is in this connection that they are of such value, as they make it possible to see at a glance whether any particular rifle is likely to prove a safe weapon for use against elephant or similar animals in thick cover. But they must not be used when expanding bullets on soft-skinned game are being considered ; other than in the case of knocking down a lion at very close quarters, when bullet weight is of far greater importance than velocity.

I must also express my very real thanks to Capt. C. R. S. Pitman, Game Warden of Uganda ; to F. G. Banks, Game Ranger of Uganda ; to the Game Warden of Kenya ; and to Capt. Phillip Teare, Game Warden of Tanganyika for their kindness and courtesy to one who was an utter and complete stranger to them.

I have also to acknowledge the courteous kindness of the Editors of the *American Rifleman*, the *Field* and of *Game and Gun* for granting me permission to work into the following pages parts of various articles, etc., of mine which, either in a somewhat similar, or entirely different, form have, from time to time, appeared in those excellent journals.

I should like to make it perfectly clear, here and now in the commencement, that I have no financial connection of any sort or description whatsoever with any firm of gunsmiths or ammunition manufacturers. What praise I have to bestow upon, or criticism to make of, any particular rifle is based solely and entirely on the merits or otherwise of those particular weapons.

I have endeavoured to deal with my subject and discuss the rifles as impartially as possible, but I am only human and if I have let myself go a little now and again, it is simply because of the intense pleasure and satisfaction that I have always derived from using certain rifles built by certain firms, and I trust that you who read will bear this fact in mind and make allowances.

JOHN TAYLOR.

PORTUGUESE EAST AFRICA,
    SEPTEMBER 1945.

CONTENTS

ABBREVIATIONS

B.P.	Black Powder.
D.B.	Double Barrelled.
F./s.	Foot-seconds.
Ft.-lb.	Foot-pounds.
H.V.	High Velocity.
L.V.	Low Velocity.
M.E.	Muzzle Energy.
M.V.	Muzzle Velocity.
S.B.	Single Barrelled.

BIG GAME AND BIG GAME RIFLES

CHAPTER I

Definitions and Details of Rifles

IN the days of black powder, sporting rifles were divided into three groups : Large Bores, Expresses and Miniatures. With the introduction of smokeless powders, however, those old definitions proved inadequate. Various attempts have been made to coin new definitions which would include the old black-powder weapons ; but I contend that that is only unnecessarily complicating matters. Black-powder rifles have ·been so completely superseded by their modern nitro-firing counterparts, that they are no longer used in Africa, and therefore I see no necessity for including them in modern definitions : if a man wishes to refer to them, then let him definitely mention " Black Powder " when doing so. This will avoid any possibility of a misunderstanding.

I venture to suggest, then, that the following definitions, which are those generally used in Africa, be adopted (they are those, at any rate, which I shall be using in the following pages) :

Large Bore.
   A rifle the calibre of which is not less than ·450.
Large Medium Bore.
   A rifle the calibre of which is not less than ·400 nor greater than ·440 (11·2 mm.).
Medium Bore.
   A rifle the calibre of which is not less than ·300 nor greater than ·375.

Small Bore.

A rifle the calibre of which is less than ·300.

Magnum.

The word "magnum" after the bore (i.e. ·375 magnum) denotes a rifle the velocity of which is not less than 2,500 f./s.

Miniature.

Any rifle having a muzzle energy of less than 1,500 ft.-lb.

Before we can satisfactorily discuss rifles suitable for any particular purpose, it is essential that we run as briefly as possible over the various problems involved.

As I have stated in the Preface, it is no purpose of mine to delve deeply into the theoretical side of the question ; nevertheless, there are certain aspects, connected with ballistics, which cannot be entirely ignored. For instance :

PRESSURE

Now the pressures developed by different rifles firing different cartridges, the ballistics of which may be very similar, can vary enormously. And there are certain very definite and very serious drawbacks to excessive pressure ; not the least being the fact that the brass cartridge case may be expanded to such an extent that it is very liable to jam in the chamber of the rifle, or, if not actually jam, at least render extraction considerably more difficult, which, in the case of a magazine or single-loader, would delay the firing of a second shot. And that delay might easily have disastrous consequences. In addition to which, of course, there is always the possibility of the action being strained.

But, although the pressure may not be sufficiently excessive to bring about any of the above conditions, there are other and much commoner disadvantages.

All nitro powders, particularly Cordite, are sensitive to variations in temperature : the higher the temperature

the more violent the combustion ; and the more violent
the combustion, the higher the pressure developed.   Consequently, if cartridges are exposed to the heat of the
sun, by carrying them in cartridge-belts round the waist
or in bandoliers over the shoulder, as one so frequently
sees being done, it is inevitable that they will generate
much higher pressures than would cartridges which had
been carried in a small pouch or in the pocket.   In the
same way, if you are out in the sun during the midday
heat, the barrels of your rifles will become so hot that you
cannot grasp them tightly with the naked hand ; which
means that the cartridges in the chambers will also
become superheated, and must be drawn and others
substituted from time to time.

And there are two serious results which follow on
this higher pressure : The first, and most immediately
noticeable, is the increase in the severity of the recoil ;
whilst the second is, in all probability, a wild shot owing
to the increase in velocity which must follow on the
higher pressure.   Because, if a cartridge is designed to
give a certain velocity with a certain pressure, if the
pressure is increased, either by reducing the air-space in
the cartridge by pushing the bullet farther down the neck
of the case or by subjecting the powder to a high temperature, the velocity *must* be increased.   Consequently, since
your rifle is sighted for a given weight of bullet and a
certain velocity, if by any means the velocity is altered,
then the rifle would need to be re-sighted if it is to be
expected to shoot accurately with the new velocity.

I remember a 10·75 mm. Mauser of German origin
that I was once using with ammunition hailing from the
same source.   I frequently noticed that on three or four
shots being fired, those cartridges which had remained
in the magazine had had the bullets driven almost out
of sight down the necks of the cartridge cases.   This, of
course, was caused by the inertia of the cartridges which,
acting against the backward movement of the rifle under

the shock of discharge, caused them to tap sharply against the front of the magazine box. The result of this was that if it was necessary for me to fire several shots in rapid succession, the pressure of each successive cartridge must have been considerably higher than was that of its predecessors and, consequently, its velocity must have been greater. And the discomfort which I suffered from the excessive recoil, and the discoloration of my shoulder, left no possible doubt as to what was happening.

The trouble was, of course, that the necks of the cartridge-cases had not been swedged or pinched into the cannelures of the bullets; in fact, some of the bullets had no cannelure. (The " cannelure " is the groove near the base of a bullet and is there for the purpose of having the neck of the case pressed into it to hold the bullet firmly in position.)

I had not had as much experience of such matters then as I have now, and could not understand why I would occasionally miss for no apparent reason at all. It must be admitted, however, that the loss in accuracy owing to the altered trajectory of the bullet is not very great; the real cause of the wild shot is more directly due to the " flip " of the barrel and its effect on the bullet, the velocity of which has now been altered.

" Flip " is the technical term used to denote the bending of the barrel under the shock of discharge and whilst the bullet is travelling up the bore. It may be likened to the action of the top portion of an angler's rod when he " strikes " his fish. Flip, or rather its effect, is counterbalanced by the gunsmith when he is sighting the rifle in the first instance. He does so by determining the exact position of the muzzle of the barrel, during its bending movement, when the bullet emerges. It sounds very intricate, but in actual practice it is quite a simple process, and one into which we need not enter here.

The point is, that he is determining the position of the muzzle for a certain weight of bullet travelling at a given velocity. Obviously, therefore, if that velocity is altered, the sighting will also need to be altered. Speaking in ordinary, every day language, the reason for this is to be found in the fact that the faster the bullet travels up the bore, the sooner it leaves the muzzle, and, since the muzzle is moving round the arc of a circle, it will be immediately obvious that two bullets travelling at different speeds must leave the bore when the muzzle of the barrel is in two different positions, since the bullet travelling at the lower velocity will remain longer in the bore and, therefore, must be affected to a greater extent by the flip.

And here may be mentioned a point which is of extreme importance, and which I have frequently been called upon to elucidate. I have, time and again, had men come to me in despair because the accuracy of their rifles, which had hitherto been beyond reproach, had now for apparently no reason at all, hopelessly fallen off. They would complain that the rifle was shooting all over the place—foot or more out.

It invariably transpired that it was only since they had been using a new consignment of ammunition that they had any complaint. Now the majority of magnum-medium and small-bore rifles fire at least two and some-times three different weights of bullet, all at different velocities. But there is only one rifle which is actually and definitely designed to fire these different weights of bullet with the same sighting, and that is Holland's ·375 magnum. All the others are only sighted for one or other of the cartridges obtainable. Therefore, if you want, for any reason, to fire one of the different weights of bullet than that for which your rifle is sighted, it is necessary for you to have the rifle re-sighted for that particular bullet and its velocity.

Consequently, when ordering a fresh consignment of ammunition, it is imperative for you to state the bullet weight for which your rifle is sighted. (It is, almost invariably in the case of a good-quality weapon, marked

2

on the barrel). Further, to avoid any possibility of a mistake and consequent disappointment, you should also state the length of case and whether it is flanged or rimless, the powder charge, velocity and any other particulars which occur to you. For instance : there are no less than 7 different cartridges for rifles of ·375-bore (not counting the 3 different bullets of each of the ·375 magnum cartridges). There are 3 different cartridges for rifles of ·400-bore, excluding the old black-powder cartridges. The ·318, ·333, and ·404 rifles all fire 2 different cartridges, whilst the ·333 can also be had as flanged or rimless.

Whilst there are as many as 10 different ·450-bore rifle cartridges, apart from the various bullets fired by some of the old black-powder patterns. There are several ·500's, and also several ·577's.

So that from the above it will be readily appreciated how important it is to give every smallest detail of the cartridges when ordering a fresh consignment.

All barrels are subject to flip, and the longer and thinner the barrel, naturally, the more pronounced the effect.

A further disadvantage of a high pressure is the shorter life of the barrel ; since pressure spells heat and heat, in turn, means greater wear and tear on the bore. All of which is to show why it is always advisable when deciding between any two rifles of approximately similar bore, weight, velocity and power, the ballistics and trajectory of which are more or less the same, to choose the one which develops the lower chamber pressure.

RECOIL

This is another ballistic element which deserves short mention. There are several factors which affect the recoil of a rifle and the extent to which it is felt. Weight, of course, is the first ; since the force that pushes the rifle back can, obviously, push a light weapon back more easily than it can one which is appreciably heavier. And it is for this reason that powerful rifles must be built up to a certain weight even as single-loaders ; if they were built very light the recoil would be entirely excessive. Some men are more sensitive to recoil than others, and to these I would tender the advice that they do not have their rifles built too light. You seldom feel recoil when actually firing at game ; but that does not mean to say that you may not experience unpleasant after-effects next day. Personally, I have always suffered far more from the recoil of a very light small bore than ever I have from a powerful, heavy, elephant rifle. Admittedly, the recoil of a ·600 is heavier than that of a ·256, its power-to-weight ratio is much greater—the ·600 is about 10 times as powerful as a ·256, but is little more than twice as heavy. And this brings me to the question of balance and fit.

Any two rifles of equal weight firing the same cartridge must have exactly the same recoil, since the power that drives the weapon back is the same in each case. But an ill-fitting, badly balanced weapon requires a considerable effort to hold it at the shoulder and keep the sights in line, which means that the muscles are tensed and strained and so transmit every particle of the recoil to the firer's body ; whereas, a perfectly-balanced, perfectly-fitting weapon requires no effort at all to hold it at the shoulder, and therefore the muscles are not tensed and hard and so act as cushions and absorb the recoil. If you fire a fairly-powerful rifle from the prone position and do not fit the butt properly into your shoulder, it will probably catch you on the collar-bone and you will know all about it next day. But if you fire the same rifle from the kneeling position, it cannot possibly catch you on the collar-bone in the same way, and there will be no unpleasant after-effects. Yet the recoil of the rifle was exactly the same. This is just to make it perfectly clear that although the recoil of any two rifles may be exactly the same, it can be felt to a far greater extent in one than in the other under certain circumstances. And, since sporting rifles are rarely fired from the prone position, the question of balance and fit can become a very large one indeed of those " circumstances "

VELOCITY

Velocity, as far as the practical sportsman is concerned, is undoubtedly the most important of the ballistic elements. Gunmakers invariably quote the muzzle velocity of each rifle in their catalogues. This, of course, denotes the velocity of the bullet as it leaves the muzzle of the barrel.

The muzzle velocity tells you several things about the rifle. The first is that it gives you an idea as to what you may expect in the way of trajectory. Other things being equal, the higher the velocity the flatter the trajectory. But a bullet encounters tremendous resistance when travelling through the air, both at its nose and also suction at its tail. The three factors that govern a bullet's capacity for overcoming this resistance are : weight, shape and diameter ; and the better the combination of these three factors in the bullet's design, the better can the bullet retain its velocity and, therefore, the flatter its trajectory curve.

The advantages of a flat trajectory are so tremendous, and so obvious, that they surely require no emphasis from me. For, in big game hunting, one of the greatest difficulties which the sportsman had to overcome, prior to the introduction of the high-velocity rifle, was the question of estimating the range. With a low-velocity rifle it was absolutely imperative to alter the sights for different ranges ; and the trouble was to determine those distances accurately. For, as any man who has ever done any big game shooting can tell you, there are times when the animals appear to be much closer than in reality they are : it is as though you were looking at them through a telescope. But, by precisely the same token, there are also occasions—and these are infinitely the more frequent —when the beasts seem to be at least double the distance away that they really are ; it is now as though you were looking at them through that same telescope, but—from the wrong end of it.

No matter how long you may live in the bush, and no matter how much you shoot, you will never learn to estimate distances correctly under all conditions.   Light has a great deal to say in the matter ; the density or otherwise of the atmosphere has a bearing on the question ; whether or not there is much moisture about must be taken into consideration ; but, by far the most important, is the type of country.   Although I hunt twelve months a year there are, nevertheless, times innumerable when I am utterly and completely fogged— when for the life of me I could not tell to within 50 or 75 paces the distance away from me that an animal was standing.   And this is where the tremendous advantage of a flat trajectory makes itself felt.   For with a low- or comparatively low-velocity rifle, that matter of the fifty-odd paces might easily make all the difference between placing your bullet where you want it, and killing cleanly—and just failing to do so.   But with a high-velocity rifle, it would make no difference.   You would just take the normal aim, and granting that you were holding your rifle steadily, the result would be the same whether the animal was 50 or 250 yards away.

One frequently hears the argument that for men who hunt mostly in fairly-close country a flat trajectory is unnecessary owing to the short ranges at which they generally fire.   But to my mind, these are just the men who are really going to thoroughly appreciate the flat trajectory.   Because if, as is probably the case, they do not fire more than half a dozen shots a year at ranges in excess of 150 yards, then surely they will have infinitely greater difficulty in estimating the range for those occasional longish shots than would a man who does most of his shooting at ranges varying between 150 and 250 yards ?

The second great advantage of a high velocity is that, provided the bullet has been properly designed so that it will retain that initial velocity (and this you can tell by a glance at its trajectory curve), then obviously it will have a high striking velocity. That is, that it will be travelling at a high speed when it strikes the animal at which you are firing.

Now where soft-skinned game are concerned, a high striking velocity is a very great advantage ; and this for two reasons : The first is, that the higher the striking velocity, the more readily will an expanding bullet set up ; which means that a somewhat heavier bullet can be used, and consequently a heavier blow inflicted on that score alone.

The second reason is, the higher the striking velocity the greater the shock transmitted to the muscles and tissues surrounding the part struck as the expanding bullet sets up. An animal shot through the heart with a low-velocity bullet will gallop off at full speed for anything up to 100 yards or more before collapsing. But, if a high-velocity bullet had been used, that same animal would in all probability have dropped stone dead in its tracks precisely as though it had been shot through the brain or had had its neck broken. And this even if the heart had been missed, provided that the bullet had struck within reasonable distance of it.

For the shock of a high-velocity bullet seems to have a paralysing effect on the muscles and tissues surrounding the point of impact ; which spells instantaneous death to an animal if the bullet strikes anywhere within reasonable distance of the heart. The advantages of this can readily be seen if we take the case of four or five lions having a feed in the open at a range of, say, 100 paces. There is a clump of long grass just beyond them.

If you open fire with a low-velocity magazine rifle,

you may be able to put a bullet into each one of them.
You may think, and feel pretty sure, that all five shots
were sufficiently well placed to kill ; but, assuming that
you took heart shots, all five lions will have bounded
away and probably disappeared in the grass.   You will
have to follow them up.   Now there are pleasanter things
in life than entering a clump of grass which may be
harbouring five more-or-less-badly-wounded lions !
Two or three of them may, and probably will, be dead ;
but you cannot tell for certain until you find them.   One
wounded lion at a time in a clump of grass is enough
for the average man ; two is a surfeit for a glutton.   But
a possible, if not probable, five !

But had you been using a high-velocity magnum rifle,
those same lions—assuming that the bullets were all
equally well placed—would have collapsed then and there
before ever they reached that clump of grass.

I have frequently had men boast that their low-velocity
rifles were more powerful than my high-velocity magnum
because they had succeeded in driving an expanding bullet
clean through an animal, whereas my bullet had invariably
remained in the animal's body.   Such men do not seem
to realize that in driving a bullet right through an animal's
body a considerable proportion of the power is being
wasted in the ground, tree, ant-hill, or whatever it is that
eventually stops the bullet.   It was principally for this
reason that expanding bullets were invented.   Admittedly
an expanding bullet, even if it does go right through an
animal, inflicts a much more deadly wound than does a
solid, since, apart from the fact that on setting up it
becomes at least twice as big as it originally was, it also
becomes a jagged affair, and consequently does vastly
more damage.   But if the animal is to receive the full force
of the blow, it is imperative that the bullet should remain
in its body.

If you stand a bag of oats up on a tree-stump and prod
it with a rapier, you will not knock it over ; but if you

try to drive a walking-stick through it, you will upset it
—simply because it has stopped the stick and therefore
received the full force of the stroke ; whereas the rapier
just snicked through.

But no greater mistake can be made than to rush to
velocity whilst ignoring bullet weight. Because the
higher the striking velocity the more readily will an
expanding bullet set up. Consequently, if a very light
bullet with a very high velocity is used against one of
the larger varieties of soft-skinned game, it will blow to
pieces all too readily, particularly should it happen to
encounter a bone ; probably inflicting a tremendous
surface wound but failing to do anything like the damage
inside that it ought to do. For instance, there is a positive
mania amongst sportsmen in Africa for very light small-
bore rifles. In days gone by such weapons, used with
the old low-velocity ammunition and somewhat heavier
bullets, were reasonably satisfactory ; but today, with the
new high-velocity ammunition and very light bullets, they
are only intended for use against the very lightest varieties
of soft-skinned game. Yet men use them on animals
weighing up to three-quarters of a ton or so, and then
complain that the bullets break up too soon ! They say
that they want a rifle firing inexpensive ammunition for
non-dangerous game, as the ammunition for their more
powerful weapons is too costly ; but they appear to over-
look the fact that they frequently have to fire, perhaps,
three or four of those cheaper cartridges into an animal
to kill it, whereas one shot from a powerful rifle would
have been sufficient.

Therefore, when deciding on any particular rifle or
bullet, consideration must be given to the type of animal
most likely to be encountered.

ENERGY

Now theorists may declare that energy is a perfectly
accurate mathematical measurement of a rifle's power at

any given range. There can be no doubt that it is a perfectly accurate mathematical measurement, but I utterly fail to see what use it is to the practical sportsman; for the excellent reason that it does not give a basis from which a comparison of any two rifles can be made with any real degree of accuracy. Gunsmiths, of course, invariably quote it in their catalogues because, particularly nowadays since the introduction of the magnum high-velocity rifle, it is decidedly flattering to their weapons.

To explain what I mean by saying that energy does not permit of a fair comparison being made, let us take the excellent example of the ·404. Now the standard cartridge for this rifle fires a 400-grain bullet with a velocity of 2,125 f./s. which shows a muzzle energy of 4,020 ft.-lb.; but the high-velocity cartridge throws a 300-grain bullet with a velocity of 2,600 f./s. which in turn shows a theoretical mathematical muzzle energy of 4,500 ft.-lb. From this, any uninitiated sportsman might well be excused for believing that the 300-grain bullet strikes a heavier blow than does the 400-grain bullet. But this is not the case. Granting that a high striking velocity is an advantage where soft-skinned game are concerned at medium and long ranges; when it comes to close-quarter work against dangerous game, bullet weight is essential. Within reasonable limits it can be stated that the heavier the bullet the heavier the blow delivered. Theoretical energy lays too much stress on velocity at the expense of bullet weight.

The difference, of course, between these two cartridges is not very great; but to take an exaggerated example: The 143-grain bullet from a ·280 Halger at 300 yards shows a theoretical energy greater than that of the 750-grain bullet from a ·577 at the same range. But if the 750-grain bullet from the ·577 hit an elephant in the head at that range, but missed the brain, it would knock him down, whereas if the 143-grain bullet from the ·280

Halger missed the brain by the same amount it would have no effect on the elephant whatsoever. Admittedly this is a somewhat far-fetched example ; but it frequently happens that an exaggeration of this description, by emphasizing a point, enables a man to grasp it more readily, through seeing it more easily, than if the examples were not so widely separated.

Theoretical mathematical muzzle energy is the most misleading thing in the world and should on no account be used when comparing any two rifles other than those of approximately the same bore, firing bullets of approximately the same weight ; then, perhaps, it is of some use.

In the following tables of ballistics I have given a column of figures which I have headed " Knock-Out Blow ". Now I am fully aware that the great majority of ballistic experts would look very much askance at these, but I do not care because I do not pretend that they denote killing power. Innumerable formulæ have, from time to time, been put forward to indicate a rifle's killing power, but none of them is of much value, for, as Major Burrard so concisely puts it : " The real truth is that it is impossible to express Life in mathematical terms of X, Y and Z." Nobody realizes that fact better than I do ; but I do consider that some means is desirable of enabling inexperienced sportsmen to compare any two rifles, even of widely differing bores, from the point of view of the actual blow delivered by the bullet on heavy, massive-boned animals such as elephant. This to enable them to see at a glance whether or not a rifle is likely to be a safe, suitable, and reasonably satisfactory weapon for use at close quarters in thick cover. And, since theoretical energy lays too much stress and importance on velocity and therefore cannot be relied upon for the purpose of comparison, I have worked out these values which, in my experience, approximate in an altogether remarkable way with the actual performance of the different rifles and different bullets under practical sporting conditions.

LARGE-BORE RIFLES

Rifle.	Weight of Bullet in grains.	Pressure in tons per square inch.	Velocity in ft. per sec.				Energy in ft.-lb.				Knock-Out Blow.	Approximate Weight of Rifle in pounds.	
			Muzzle.	100 yd.	200 yd.	300 yd.	Muzzle.	100 yd.	200 yd.	300 yd.	Values.	D.B.	S.B.
·600	900	14·0	1,950	1,690	1,450	1,250	7,610	5,720	4,210	3,130	150·4	14½–17	12–13
·577	750	14·0	2,050	1,730	1,450	1,210	7,020	5,000	3,510	2,440	126.7	11½–14	11
·505 Gibbs . .	525	15·0	2,300	2,020	1,790	1,550	6,180	4,760	3,740	2,810	86·25	—	10½–11
·500 Rimless . .	535	16(?)	2,400	—	—	—	6,800	—	—	—	90·3	—	10¼
·500 3¼″ . . .	570	15·5	2,125	1,880	1,650	1,440	5,730	4,490	3,450	2,640	86·5	10½–12	9–10
·476	520	16·0	2,100	1,890	1,680	1,490	5,100	4,130	3,260	2,570	74·2	11	9½
·475 No. 2 . .	480	15·5	2,200	1,960	1,730	1,510	5,170	4,100	3,200	2,440	71·7	11–12	10½
·475 No. 2 Jeffery.	500	?	2,000	1,818	—	—	4,450	3,670	—	—	67·8	11–12	10½
·475	480	15·0	2,175	1,930	1,700	1,490	5,030	3,970	3,090	2,360	70·8	11–12	10½
·470	500	14·0	2,125	1,910	1,700	1,500	5,030	4,060	3,210	2,500	71·3	10½–11½	9–10
·465	480	14·0	2,125	1,920	1,720	1,530	4,820	3,940	3,150	2,500	67·7	10¼–10¾	9–10
·450 No. 2 . .	480	13·0	2,175	1,900	—	—	5,050	3,700	—	—	67·1	10½–11½	9–10
·500/·450 . . .	480	15·5	2,175	1,990	—	—	5,050	4,220	—	—	67·1	10¼–11½	9–10
·450	480	17·0	2,150	1,960	—	—	4,930	4,100	—	—	66·3	11–11½	9–10

LARGE MEDIUM-BORE RIFLES

Rifle.	Weight of Bullet in grains.	Pressure in tons per square inch.	Velocity in ft. per sec.				Energy in ft.-lb.				Knock-Out Blow.	Approximate Weight of Rifle in pounds.	
			Muzzle.	100 yd.	200 yd.	300 yd.	Muzzle.	100 yd.	200 yd.	300 yd.	Values.	D.B.	S.B.
·440 (11·2 mm.) . . .	332	15·0	2,450	2,170	1,650	1,430	4,430	3,480	2,010	1,510	51·1	—	8½
·425 (10·75 mm.) . .	410	18·5	2,350	2,120	1,910	1,710	5,010	4,100	3,330	2,660	58·5	10½-11	9
·423 (10·75 mm.) . .	347	14·5	2,200	1,950	1,710	1,500	3,750	2,940	2,260	1,740	46·1	—	7½
·416	410	17·0	2,350	2,150	1,960	1,780	5,010	4,220	3,500	2,900	57·25	—	9¼
·405	300	17·0	2,200	1,940	1,690	1,470	3,240	2,510	1,910	1,450	38·2	—	8
·404	300	16·0	2,600	2,360	2,130	1,900	4,500	3,720	3,030	2,400	45·0	—	8½-9
·404	400	16·0	2,125	1,930	1,750	1,580	4,020	3,310	2,730	2,200	49·0	—	8½-9
·400 Jeffery . . .	400	16·0	2,125	1,940	1,760	1,590	4,010	3,350	2,760	2,250	48·6	9½-10¼	8½-9
·400 3¼" . . .	400	16·5	2,150	1,960	1,780	1,610	4,110	3,410	2,820	2,300	49·1	9½-10¼	8½-9

MAGNUM MEDIUM-BORE RIFLES

Rifle.	Weight of Bullet in grains.	Pressure in tons per square inch.	Velocity in ft. per sec.				Energy in ft.-lb.				Knock-Out Blow.	Approximate Weight of Rifle in pounds.	
			Muzzle.	100 yd.	200 yd.	300 yd.	Muzzle.	100 yd.	200 yd.	300 yd.	Values.	D.B.	S.B.
·375 Magnum	235	17·0	2,800	2,510	2,220	1,950	4,100	3,300	2,580	1,990	—	9½	8½
·375 ,, ...	270	18·0	2,650	2,430	2,210	2,000	4,220	3,550	2,930	2,400	—	9½	8½
·375 ,, ...	300	18·0	2,500	2,300	2,110	1,920	4,160	3,530	2,960	2,460	40·1	9½	8½
·369 Purdey	270	17·0	2,620	2,400	2,190	1,970	4,120	3,460	2,880	2,330	—	10	—
·350 Magnum	225	17·5	2,600	2,360	2,120	1,880	3,380	2,790	2,250	1,770	29·25	9¼	8¼
·333	250	18·0	2,500	2,300	2,120	1,930	3,470	2,940	2,500	2,070	—	9–9½	8–8½
·330 B.S.A.	165	18·0	3,000	2,700	2,410	2,130	3,300	2,680	2,140	1,670	—	—	8¾
·318	180	19·0	2,700	2,440	2,190	1,930	2,920	2,390	1,920	1,490	—	9¼	7¼–8
·318	250	19·5	2,400	2,210	2,030	1,850	3,200	2,720	2,290	1,910	27·25	9¼	7¼–8
·311 (7·9 mm.)	154	18·0	2,800	2,550	2,290	2,040	2,700	2,240	1,810	1,430	—	—	7–7½
·303 Sporting	150	18·5	2,700	2,480	2,230	2,000	2,430	2,050	1,660	1,340	—	9	7–8
·375/·300 (Super-Thirty).	150	18·5	3,000	2,750	2,510	2,270	3,000	2,520	2,100	1,720	—	9	7½–8
·375/·300 (Super-Thirty).	180	18·5	2,700	2,500	2,300	2,100	2,920	2,500	2,110	1,780	—	9	7½–8
·300 Springfield ('06) . .	150	20·0	2,700	2,460	2,220	1,980	2,440	2,020	1,640	1,310	—	—	7½–8
·300 Springfield ('06) . .	180	20·0	2,500	2,300	2,100	1,930	2,500	2,120	1,770	1,490	—	—	7½–8

MEDIUM-BORE RIFLES

Rifle.	Weight of Bullet in grains.	Pressure in tons per square inch.	Velocity in ft. per sec.				Energy in ft.-lb.				Knock-Out Blow.	Approximate Weight of Rifle in pounds.	
			Muzzle.	100 yd.	200 yd.	300 yd.	Muzzle.	100 yd.	200 yd.	300 yd.	Values.	D.B.	S.B.
·375	270	14·5	2,000	1,790	1,600	1,420	2,400	1,920	1,540	1,220	28·9	9–9½	8–8½
·400/·375	270	—	2,175	1,930	—	—	2,840	2,235	—	—	31·5	9–9½	8–8½
·375 (9·5 mm. Mann-Schon.)	270	17·0	2,250	2,040	1,830	1,630	3,030	2,500	2,010	1,590	32·5	—	7½–8½
·366 (9·3 mm. Mauser) .	285	16·5	2,175	1,960	1,760	1,570	3,000	2,440	1,960	1,570	32·8	—	7½
·360 No. 2	320	14·7	2,200	2,110	1,830	1,660	3,450	3,170	2,390	1,970	36·2	9–10	8–9
·360 Westley Richards .	314	15·5	1,900	1,720	1,550	1,390	2,520	2,060	1,680	1,350	30·7	9	8
·400/·360	300	15·5	1,950	1,760	1,580	1,410	2,540	2,070	1,670	1,330	30·1	9	8
·355 (9 mm. Mauser) . .	245	17·0	2,150	1,920	1,700	1,500	2,520	2,000	1,580	1,230	26·7	—	7–7½
·355 (9 mm. Mann-Schon.)	245	17·0	2,100	1·870	1,660	1,460	2,400	1,900	1,500	1,160	26·1	—	7–7½
·400/·350	310	16·0	2,150	1,970	1,790	1,630	3,190	2,680	2,210	1,820	33·3	9	8
·350 Winchester . . .	250	17·0	2,200	1,970	1,760	1,550	2,690	2,160	1,720	1,340	—	—	7½–8
·333	300	18·5	2,200	2,030	1,860	1,700	3,240	2,750	2,310	1,930	31·4	9¼	8–8½
·318	250	19·5	2,400	2,210	2,030	1,850	3,200	2,720	2,290	1,910	27·25	9¼	7¼–8
·315 (8 mm. Mann-Schon.)	200	14·0	2,200	1,970	1,750	1,540	2,160	1,730	1,360	1,060	—	—	6½–7½
·315 (8 mm. Mannlicher).	244	14·0	2,025	1,840	1,670	1,500	2,230	1,840	1,520	1,220	22·4	—	7–7½
·315 (8-mm. Lebel) . .	198	14·0	2,300	2,100	1,910	1,730	2,330	1,940	1,610	1,320	—	—	7–8
·303 Mark VI	215	16·5	2,060	1,870	1,680	1,510	2,030	1,680	1,360	1,050	19·2	9	7–8
·303 Sporting	192	17·0	2,200	1,980	1,770	1,570	2,060	1,670	1,340	1,050	—	9	7–8
·303 Mark VII	174	18·5	2,450	2,250	2,060	1,850	2,320	1,960	1,640	1,320	—	9	7–8
·303 Savage	180	17·0	1,975	1,750	1,550	1,350	1,560	1,230	860	730	—	—	7
·375/·300 (Super-Thirty) .	220	18·5	2,350	2,170	2,000	1,830	2,700	2,300	1,960	1,640	22·15	9	7½–8
·300 Springfield ('o6) . .	220	20·0	2,200	2,020	1,850	1,690	2,370	2,000	1,680	1,400	20·7	—	7½–8
·311 (7·9-mm. Mauser) .	227	15·5	2,025	1,830	1,640	1,460	2,060	1,590	1,360	1,040	20·4	—	7–7½
·311 (7·9-mm. Mauser) .	244	16·5	2,030	1,850	1,670	1,500	2,240	1,860	1,510	1,210	22·0	—	7–7½

They *do* give an excellent basis for comparison from the point of view of the actual blow delivered, and allow the large bore with its heavy bullet and reasonable velocity to come into its own and not be overshadowed by high velocity.

No better example of this can be found than in the case of the ·465- and ·416-bore rifles: If you take a frontal head shot at an elephant with a ·416 and miss the brain, you will not stun him other than momentarily—in all probability his hindquarters will give way, and he will squat there like a huge pig for a few moments then, if you don't finish him off at once, will heave to his feet, swing round and clear off; but had you taken the same shot with a ·465, the elephant would have been knocked out entirely. The theoretical mathematical energy of the ·416 is somewhat greater than that of the ·465, but the bullet is considerably lighter. My " Knock-Out " values show the ·465 to hit a heavier blow than the ·416. I am fully aware that the ·416 hits a sufficiently heavy blow for all practical purposes, but that is an entirely different story ; the point that I wish to make is that my figures show the true difference that there is between these two rifles from the point of view of the actual blow delivered—as proved by actual experience in the bush— whereas theoretical energy would seem to show that the ·416 is the more powerful weapon.

It must be clearly understood, however, that they really only apply to bluff-nosed, solid bullets used against heavy, massive-boned animals. Theoretical energy probably gives a surer indication when expanding bullets on soft-skinned animals are concerned. I have only worked out the values for small-bore high-velocity rifles because of certain men who used to use small-bore rifles for elephant, though they are rarely used nowadays. But the books which these men wrote are still extant and young beginners might very easily be persuaded after reading them that small-bore rifles are all that are necessary. However, a glance at these values and a look through the chapter dealing with elephant should, I think, prove pretty con· clusively that they are by no means all that are necessary.

The following tables are by no means complete, but they show all the principal rifles built by British manu- facturers, and all the rifles in general use in Africa at the present day.

A study of the above tables will more than repay the small effort required. Where the " K-O " values are not given it is because the bullets for the cartridges concerned are obtainable in pointed form only. I have worked out the " K-O " value of the high-velocity 300-grain bullet for the ·404 to show how, had it been a bluff-nosed bullet, it would not have inflicted so heavy a blow as does the standard 400-grain bullet.

ACTIONS

There are really only two main types of rifle in general use in Africa nowadays : Double-barrelled and Single-barrelled with Magazine. Nevertheless, there is a third type—the Single-barrelled, Single-loader—con- cerning which I shall have something to say anon.

It is not necessary here to go into the various problems involved in the building of double rifles ; suffice it to say that cheap doubles should be left severely alone. If you cannot afford a new best-quality double, then get a second-hand one. If you buy it from the original makers, their guarantee will go with it and, consequently, it can be absolutely relied upon. No first-class firm would sell you a " pup " ; it would be more than their reputation is worth. Remember, there are many wealthy sportsmen who have a first-class battery of rifles built for them. They come out here to Africa, spend three months or so in the bush and then go home again, quite possibly to remain there. As often as not, such men have had their fill of big game hunting and hand their rifles over to their gunmakers to sell for them. Now these rifles have only had a very few shots fired through them and, for all practical purposes, may be considered as being brand new ; yet in all probability you could pick them up for not more than two-thirds or thereabouts of their original cost. And, what is more, such rifles will be a vastly better investment than new cheaper-quality weapons at approximately the same figure.

As I have already stated, I do not wish to become theoretical, but there are various problems involved in the adjustment of the barrels of a double so that both barrels will place their shots in the same group. And when it is borne in mind that the increase in velocity consequent upon the higher temperatures which must inevitably result from taking the rifle and its ammunition to the tropics must in turn result in a variation of the grouping powers of the two barrels, all of which has to be foreseen and counteracted by the gunsmith in England, it will be readily appreciated that great skill and much time must be spent on the adjustment of those barrels. Obviously, therefore, a cheap weapon cannot possibly have had the same time spent on it, or it could not be sold at such a low figure—quite apart from the workmanship and material used for the locks and action.

Magazine rifles are vastly less expensive to build ; whilst the sighting of a single-barrelled weapon is a very simple matter compared with the adjustment of a double. But, no matter which type you are considering, get the very highest quality that you can possibly afford.

COMPARISON OF DOUBLE AND MAGAZINE RIFLES

One is frequently asked the question : Which ought I to get ? And really it is a most difficult question to answer ; so much has to be taken into consideration ; not the least being the question of cost. But leaving that on one side ; broadly speaking, the type which you prefer and in which you have the greatest confidence, is the best *for you.* Save in exceptional circumstances, whether it is a magazine or a double is entirely a matter of personal preference. The ideal battery should, perhaps, include both ; one or other being definitely preferable, though not necessarily essential, for certain types of hunting under certain conditions.

For instance, for general African shooting, which consists of killing the larger varieties of soft-skinned game at ranges varying between 75 and 175 yards and occasionally up to 250, in semi-open scrub country, the majority of men consider that a high-velocity medium-bore magazine rifle in the magnum group is definitely preferable to a double. Because in good game country, the solitary lion is very much the exception ; and if you are tackling a " bunch " of lion of anything from five or six to thirteen or fifteen or even more, the ability to fire several shots in rapid succession, if necessary, is a very decided advantage.

But when tackling dangerous game at very close quarters in very thick cover—heavy forest, dense, matted tangles of bush, thick scrub, or oceans of 10-foot " elephant " grass—the double is generally preferred. And this for two reasons :

As everybody knows, balance helps one enormously to swing and mount a rifle or gun for a quick *and accurate* snap-shot. Now no single-barrelled weapon, whether magazine or not, can ever be anything like so well balanced as a double, for the simple reason that there is not the same concentration of weight between the hands with the former as there is with the latter. Further, a double can be swung into action very much more rapidly than can a magazine. All powerful magazine rifles have a Mauser-pattern bolt action in which the safety catch must be twisted across from the right- to the left-hand side before the rifle can be fired. This operation cannot be performed whilst the rifle is being swung up to the shoulder, and consequently an appreciable amount of time must elapse before the rifle is ready for use. Whereas, with a double, the safety can be snicked forward whilst the rifle is actually being swung up to the shoulder and mounted for the shot. There is not an instant's unnecessary delay. Also, the shortness, compactness and general handiness of a double all combine to make it undoubtedly preferable in very thick cover.

Generally speaking, however, as I have already stated, it is really a matter for the individual to decide for himself. But it will be noted that I qualified that statement by the remark: " Save in exceptional circumstances ". I did so on purpose, because I consider that for two types of hunting the double-barrelled weapon is not merely preferable but is definitely and absolutely essential.

These are: When hunting in, or even travelling through, very thick bush in which rhino are numerous and, therefore, wherein you are liable to be attacked without warning or provocation from very close quarters ; and when following a wounded lion into a clump of grass or thicket of bush. Here there can be no opinions, no two possible opinions—a double-barrelled weapon should always be carried.

I remember—nor am I likely to forget—how on one occasion some years ago I was suddenly attacked by a rhino. I was not hunting, but just trekking through an area of very thick thorn-bush in which I was unaware that there were any rhino. My gun-bearer was carrying my rifle—a double—as I had trained him to do, that is : just a pace and a half in front of me so that I shall not tread on his heels, but can, if necessary, reach out a hand and grab the rifle off his shoulder ; and I insisted on his carrying it muzzle-foremost.

On this particular occasion, there was a snort and a crash in the bush on my immediate left. It was obviously a rhino, and he was much too close to be pleasant. I grabbed the rifle off the boy's shoulder and snicked forward the safety slide as the barrels fell into my left hand.

At that instant, the rhino's head broke through the bush beside me. There was no question of aiming; there was not even time in which to swing the butt up to my shoulder, for he was right on me. With the butt of the rifle on a level with my hip, and from a range of only a few inches, I fired; then I jumped to one side, turning slightly as I did so in the hope of being able to face him and give him another shot if necessary. And it was that slight twist which I gave my body that saved me from being impaled. His horn could not have missed me by much more than an inch or two, and it was the side of his broad snout that caught me under the left buttock and lifted me. He hurled me high in the air—so high that my carriers, who were following along some little distance away round a bend in the path, saw me soaring up above the thorn. I turned over in the air—not wishing to land on my back—and doubtless the heavy rifle to which I was still clinging, as a man clings to the reins when thrown over his horse's head, helped to bring me round. I came down on all fours, and my left knee struck a small, wedge-shaped outcrop of rock. I rolled over and sat up. Then, seeing the rhino's head protruding through the bush, and not knowing whether he was dead or only stunned—for the head was upright—I gave him the contents of the left barrel in the brain. My knee-cap, as I subsequently discovered, being cracked across, I was definitely " out of the running " so was taking no unnecessary chances. On hearing the second shot, my carriers came running up; for when they saw me soaring up over the bush they had not unnaturally imagined that I had fired the last shot that I was ever likely to fire.

Convinced that my knee-cap was shattered, I was terrified to move it as I dreaded confirmation of my fears. Then followed a nightmare journey to the nearest native village; fortunately there was one only about 5 miles away; though I should not care to have to undertake that 5 miles again ! With my arms round the shoulders of my two gun-bearers, I hopped and hobbled along; whenever I stubbed the foot of the injured leg against a stone or a root, I had to sit down and rest. Eventually, after I had finished the contents of my wee flask, I sat down and refused to budge another inch. Four of the strongest of my coons came back just then, however, and hoisting me to their shoulders, carried me the last mile or two to camp.

Now, on that occasion, I could not possibly have got a shot off in time from a magazine rifle. And, although I admit that I may spend the rest of my life hunting in thick cover without ever again being attacked from such very close quarters; by precisely the same token, it may happen again tomorrow. . . . You never can tell. And the longer that I live and hunt in the African bush, so the more surely do I realize that it is the unexpected that you must learn to expect.

(Yes, I know; but that is not quite such an " Irishism " as it may appear at first glance. At any rate, it exactly describes what I mean).

Then, to take the other type of hunting for which I consider that the double is so essential : following up a wounded lion.

Now practically every writer on the subject stresses the fact that you have a second shot in immediate reserve as the principal advantage of a double. I should be the last to deny the very great advantage of that quick second shot. Because, although admittedly the second shot from a magazine can be fired almost incredibly quickly with practice, there is no getting away from the fact that the bolt *must* be drawn back and then pushed forward again, and the hand returned to the grip, before the second shot can be fired. Whereas, with a double it is only necessary to slip the finger back from one trigger to the other ; and not even that if you use a single-trigger mechanism.

But, important and all as that undoubtedly is, it is not so important as the rapidity with which the first shot can be fired *with accuracy*.   Because, where dangerous game are concerned, it is the FIRST shot that counts.   The man who has not seen it with his own eyes, can have no conception of the vitality of African game.   It is no uncommon sight to see some wretched beast, shot in the belly with a dum-dum bullet, clear off and leave its entire stomach and intestines behind.   Whilst the felines appear to possess a greater vitality than any other species.

There are many more men walking about today that have stopped bullets with their bodies than was the case prior to 1914.   And many of these men can tell you that, having stopped one, if several more followed rapidly on the heels of that first one, more often than not, the recipient had not the slightest idea that he had received more than the one wound.   The shock of the first bullet seems to have a temporarily numbing effect on the nerves. And so it is with game.

I was reading not long ago how a well-known amateur hunter was describing a lion hunt in which he and two or three companions succeeded in placing no less than thirteen bullets from modern high-power rifles into a lion before they managed to bring him down.   This, of course, was because the first shot had not been vitally placed, and the succeeding shots—although had any one of them been the first it would, in all probability, have crippled him—now had apparently no effect on him whatsoever.

I, myself, personally knew two young sportsmen who between them actually succeeded in placing forty-two shots into an elephant without bringing him down.   And even after that, he was able to kill one and seriously injure the other before he, himself, collapsed.

All this to show how intensely important is the accurate placing of the first shot.   Now if you are following up a wounded lion, admittedly he has already received his first shot.   But by the time that you catch up with him, to a very great extent the first numbing effects of that shot will be wearing off; and consequently, the next which he receives will be almost as effective as if it was the actual first. But quite apart from that, if you are following him into a clump of longish grass, the advantage is all with him : he can hear you coming, whereas you have no idea as to just where he is. The instant before he charges, however, he will usually give vent to a furious, grating snarl. Now that snarl discovers his position to you, and if you are using a double, in all probability, you will be able to slam a heavy bullet into him whilst he is still a stationary target, owing to the great rapidity with which a double can be swung and mounted for a snap-shot. If the bullet was not too well placed, at least it will knock him down and so allow ample time for a second shot before he has gathered wits together sufficiently to do anything about it.

Whereas, with a magazine rifle, that first shot could not have been fired quite so quickly with the same degree of accuracy ; which means that the lion might or might not have been under way, and consequently, if he was, must have presented a very much more difficult target. This in turn means that he might not be knocked down quite so effectively and therefore would gather himself together again sooner, when a quick second shot would be essential, and you might or might not be able to get it off from the magazine in time.

Admittedly, these are both somewhat exceptional cases ; but there is no means of knowing when they are going to turn up. If you do decide on a magazine rifle, however, let nothing induce you to invest in one of those cheap, mass-production weapons, hailing from the Continent, that one sees being used on all sides in Africa. They are, each and every one of them, potential death-traps—for the user. The following extract from a letter which appeared in the correspondence columns of *Game and Gun*, is most illuminating :

. . . Your correspondent . . . puts his finger on the right spot
where all the cheap Continental rifles in general use in Africa are
concerned—their capacity for jamming.   And they generally do it at
the worst possible moment.   You may try to make them jam a thousand
times without success—and then they will let you down in a tight
corner.

A fellow-hunter shot a considerable quantity of non-dangerous game
with one, and had no trouble for some months.   He then sold it to a
friend who wounded a lion, got a jam, and his body was brought in
by his hunting-boys.

Now this exactly bears out my own experience with
rifles of this description.   I could quote numerous other
incidents of a similar nature from the experiences of other
hunters showing the utter unreliability of this type of
weapon ; but just one experience of my own should, I
think, suffice.

It was a 10·75 mm. of German origin that let me down.
I had closed a large herd of elephant in long grass up
amongst the hills on the Angoni plateau in Portuguese
East.   I spotted a magnificent tusker standing broadside
on to me at a range of only some 15 or 20 feet.   I threw
up the rifle and touched the trigger, only to be rewarded
with a dull " click ".   Careless of noise—for I badly
wanted that big chap—I whipped back the bolt and
slammed it forward again.   Subconsciously, I seemed to
feel that it moved forward suspiciously easily ; but at
the time, I did not really grasp the significance.   The
bull had heard me, of course, and had moved away, only
to pull up again some 25 yards or so farther along.   The
grass had been trampled down between us, so that I
had a clear view of him.   But on touching the trigger,
the result was the same.   The remainder of the herd were
now on the alert and were moving about restlessly, not
sure which way to run. I was right in amongst them and
had them, literally, all round me ; though I could only
see faint, shadowy shapes here and there in the grass.

The big fellow that I wanted so badly now moved off
and disappeared in the grass, and another with good teeth,

but smaller, took his place. I took a fresh cartridge from my pocket and slipped it up the spout. This went off all right and dropped the bull. On the heels of the shot there was the usual pandemonium, and I saw the first big bull run up to my right and join a small group of elephant up there, whilst the main body of the herd cleared off to the left.

I raced after the big tusker in the hope of getting a smack at him before he realized that he and his companions were being deserted by the remainder of the herd. I came on him, standing facing me, ears out and trunk down, offering a perfect frontal brain shot at a range of 25 or 30 paces. But that elephant's luck was in that day ; for my wretched rifle again only " clicked " and, on my manipulating the bolt, did the same thing again. Fortunately for me, the bull then swung round and cleared off. I was so disgusted that I hurled the rifle after him, together with some advice as to what he should do with it. . . .

On examining it later, I discovered that the magazine spring had broken ; and there was I clicking and snapping what was, to all intents and purposes, an unloaded rifle in the midst of a large herd of elephant in long grass ! The first shot had, of course, been a genuine misfire (the ammunition hailed from the same source as the rifle) and thereafter the manipulation of the bolt had been unable to reload the rifle owing to the broken magazine spring failing to push the cartridges up sufficiently to enable the bolt to grip the uppermost and carry it into the chamber. Never dreaming of such a thing happening, I did not attach enough importance to the ease with which the bolt moved forward. Now the breaking of the magazine spring like that might very easily have very serious consequences indeed.

You will do better, far, far better, to buy one good British-built rifle, than a battery of cheap, Continental weapons at the same price. The tremendous confidence which is yours when you know that there is not the slightest fear or danger of your rifles or ammunition letting you down is of incalculable benefit. Be they doubles or magazines, it matters not : Have your rifles built by one of the best London gunsmiths ; get your ammunition through them ; and you will find that your shooting and your pleasure in shooting will improve out of all recognition.

I am firmly and absolutely convinced that, at the very least, 50 per cent of what success I have had is directly due to that feeling of confidence engendered by only using the best rifles and ammunition. Since I first started using best-quality London-built rifles and ammunition, many years ago, I have used nothing else ; and I can honestly and truthfully state that I have not had a single, solitary jam, misfire, hang-fire, or weak round from that day to this.

CHAPTER II

On African Big Game Hunting Generally

I N Africa, " Big Game " should read " Dangerous
Game ". The expression " big game hunting " is
invariably used with reference to dangerous game. An
eland is the largest of all antelope and weighs upwards of
three-quarters of a ton ; but a man is not considered a
big game hunter just because he has succeeded in slaying
a couple of eland.

Africa is most decidedly the home of big game hunting,
be the game hunted dangerous or not. There is not only
more game, but there is also an infinitely greater variety
of game, to be found in Africa than in any other part of
the world.

Except for the great open plains in parts of Kenya and
Tanganyika ; generally speaking, African hunting is conducted in what may be termed semi-open scrub country.
In parts, of course, it is very much closer than in others ;
but, throughout the length and breadth of the continent,
it is mighty rarely that anybody with any pretensions to
calling himself a hunter cannot get within 200 yards of
his quarry. Occasionally, shots may have to be fired
at ranges running up to 250, or thereabouts ; but, as a
general guide, it may be taken that the average range at
which game is shot is from 75 to 175, or possibly 200,
yards. This, of course, refers to the ordinary game shooting, that is : the killing of the larger and heavier varieties
of soft-skinned animals, with which lion may be included.

Heavy, thick-skinned, massive-boned animals such as
elephant, rhino and buffalo, are shot at very much closer
ranges—particularly the first two. In fact, for elephant,
I look upon anything over 40 yards as a very long shot.
The average range at which my elephant are killed would

probably work out at somewhere between 12 and 20 paces —frequently very much less.

Soft-skinned game, excluding lion and leopard, are classed as non-dangerous ; though it is by no means unknown for certain varieties to charge when wounded, if you rush up too close when finishing them off.

The thick-skinned animals are all classed as dangerous game as also, of course, are lion.

Leopard, being encountered so very seldom in daylight, are not usually classed as anything at all ; though, in my opinion, a wounded leopard is, potentially at any rate, one of the most dangerous beasts in all Africa.

It should always be the sportsman's endeavour to get as close as ever he possibly can before opening fire.   The closer you are, the larger the animal appears and consequently the greater certainty of placing your bullet in a vital spot.   In addition, the closer you are the less scope will errors in aim or in trigger pressing have in which to develop.   Particularly does this apply to dangerous game. With any type of game, you should never fire until you can clearly see your way to make a kill.   If it is not possible to place your bullet in an immediately vital spot, then you must fire for a definitely crippling shot.   Where soft-skinned game are concerned, a body shot is permissible provided that expanding bullets are used. Thick-skinned game must be either killed outright or else crippled ; body shots are useless. (By " body-shot ", I refer to a shot too far back in the body to give any hope of finding either heart or lungs.)

Small-bore rifles are not suitable for general African use, which implies, as I have already stated, the killing of the larger varieties of soft-skinned game.   I am fully aware that small-bores are widely used in British Africa ; but that does not alter my views.   These rifles were designed and intended for use against the very lightest and softest skinned animals ; their bullets were also designed for the very rapid expansion necessary for such animals. These very light bullets can never prove other than disappointing when used against the much heavier beasts usually shot in Africa ; they inevitably tend to blow to pieces on impact should they encounter a bone. This is not the fault of the bullet, but of the man who uses it against animals so much heavier than those for which it was designed. If the old low-velocity ammunition is used in them, with the somewhat heavier bullets that it fired, if the bullet is not absolutely centrally placed, the animal will clear off and leave practically no blood spoor at all, so that it may get away altogether to die miserably perhaps days later.

For general African use any medium-bore rifle throwing a bullet of not less than 220 grains, or thereabouts, will be found most effective, though some are, of course, better than others. The rifles generally favoured are : Westley Richards ·318, Jeffery's ·333, Rigby's ·350 magnum, Purdey's ·369, Holland's ·375 magnum ; the ·366 (9·3 mm. Mauser), ·404 and ·423 (10·75 mm. Mauser) are also popular. Rifles of less power and smaller bore than the ·318, with the sole exception of Holland's " Super 30 " (·375–·300) and the American Springfield ·300, loaded in either case with the 220-grain bullet, should never be used on any but the very smallest animals in Africa. Commander D. E. Blunt, in that splendid book of his, *Elephant*, says that he would like to see a regulation in the game laws prohibiting rifles of less than ·318-bore for use in Africa ; and I should like to associate myself with him in this suggestion, for I most heartily endorse it wherein it applies to general African hunting.

Should you require a battery of rifles in a hurry and not have time to study a book of this description, or even after having read it still find yourself a trifle moidered, then my advice to you is this : Go to any one of the best London gunsmiths, tell him to what part of the world you are going, give him an idea of the *maximum* amount that you feel that you can afford, and leave yourself in his hands.   You need not have the slightest qualms about doing a thing of this description.   The best gunsmiths are a race apart ; they will not take advantage of your ignorance.   It would not pay them to do so.   Besides which, in my experience, gunsmiths take a pride in their rifles and show a definite interest in them even after they have sold them.   Remember, these men are constantly chatting with, and receiving correspondence from, sportsmen and hunters all over the world.   They know the demand that there is for certain weapons for certain purposes in various countries and districts.   Their advice is worth following.

Unless you know the man who is selling it to you, let nothing induce you to buy a second-hand rifle in Africa.   There is probably some very good reason why the owner wants to sell it !   If it is a good British-built weapon he will not be wanting to part with it.   The rifles which are constantly changing hands in Africa are those cheap, machine-made abominations of Continental origin.   Leave them severely alone.

At the risk of repeating myself—for I do not consider that it can be too strongly emphasized—I am going to again say : Buy the best, the very best, that you can possibly afford.   You will never regret it.

CHAPTER III

Rifles for Elephant Hunting

WHERE all dangerous game are concerned, the beginner should use the most powerful rifle that he can handle with comfort and ease.

The reason for this is as follows and should, I think, be fairly obvious : He will, almost certainly, thrill with excitement when for the first time he closes a herd of the biggest of all big game ; he may, quite possibly—and very excusably—feel a trifle nervous ; in the event of a charge, he may lose his head and fire wildly. Now, none of these conditions is going to help to steady him and, through him, his rifle. Consequently, he cannot be too certain of placing his shot just exactly where he wants it. Obviously, therefore, if the bullet is not too accurately placed, the heavier the blow that it delivers the greater the certainty of knocking the animal down and permitting of a second shot being fired.

The small-bore enthusiasts will tell you that, since the vital spots on an elephant are so small, a rifle with which extremely accurate shooting can be made is of primary importance. But the vital spots on an elephant are not in themselves so small ; they are only small in comparison with his bulk ; in themselves they are quite generous-sized targets. And any good rifle, double, single or magazine, will have all the accuracy necessary to enable you to place your bullets where you want them—particularly when the very close ranges at which elephant are shot is born in mind. And in spite of all that the small-bore enthusiasts may tell you, there is no getting away from the fact that no small, light bullet can be relied upon to knock down an animal if the brain is missed.

Any modern rifle, large or small, firing bluff-nosed,

solid, metal-covered bullets is capable of killing the largest elephant in Africa; but—the mere capacity to kill, *alone*, is insufficient. A ·256 will kill an elephant, provided that that elephant is sufficiently accommodating to expose a vital spot. And that is just the point.

In the dense, matted tangles of bush in which elephant are usually found nowadays, you cannot always choose your shot—in fact, it is mighty seldom that you can do so. It is frequently necessary to cripple the beast, and no light bullet can definitely be relied upon to smash massive shoulders and hips, at least not unless the bone is struck at absolute right-angles; in addition, sometimes your only chance of bagging an elephant is to stun him: the bush is so dense that you have no hope of finding the brain from the position in which you are standing and from the angle at which you must fire; if you move from there, you cannot see the brute at all. Your only hope is to knock him out. If you hit him in the head on a shot of that description with a light, or even fairly light bullet, you may knock him down but you certainly will not knock him out. I will not go so far as to say that he will bounce up again like a golf ball; but he certainly will not stay down long enough to enable you to tear your way through the tangle of bush and finish him off. Which shows at once that no small-bore can really be a suitable or satisfactory weapon for elephant, quite apart from any question of safety.

And this brings us to another important point. Now a charging elephant is a comparatively simple proposition, provided that you do not lose your head. He, almost invariably, carries his trunk rolled upwards and inwards exposing his forehead and so permits of a clean frontal brain shot. A small-bore will kill him as cleanly as a large bore. But an elephant which is stampeding directly towards you is a very different proposition. Far more often than not, his trunk is stretched up and out in front of him, blocking a frontal brain shot. And, under these circumstances, no light bullet can really and truly be relied upon to even turn the animal, much less knock him down or stop him : it may do so ; but it also may not.

But there is an even more dangerous proposition than the stampeding elephant.   When closing a herd of elephant in thick cover you are supposed to place each and every member of the herd before opening fire.   Now this sounds very well on paper, and should always be done where possible.   But it all too frequently happens in actual practice that, in dense, matted tangles of thorn bush, it is a physical impossibility to manœuvre round and place the individual beasts.   Consequently, there may be a nervous or peevish cow standing so close to you on the other side of a thick bush that you could touch her with an outstretched walking-stick, had you known that she was there and felt like doing so.   But the first intimation that you have of her existance at all is a shrill, trumpeting blast on the heels of the shot that you may have fired at some other member of the herd.   You look up and find her tusks and trunk literally right over your head.   There is no question of it being a charge ; she has not got the necessary room in which to charge.   It is just a vicious attack.   You will not have time in which to even throw the rifle to your shoulder, much less in which to aim.   It is just a case of blazing off in her face with the butt of your rifle on a level with your waist.   Since you are shooting upwards at the under side of her face, a heavy bullet is absolutely essential.   A light bullet, no matter how high its velocity, will have no effect upon her, no effect at all—except, possibly, to further infuriate her.

I have, myself, been attacked in just such a manner on several occasions, and I know, personally, several other hunters, and have heard of still more, who have been similarly attacked ; and I can most definitely and most emphatically state that no light bullet will have the slightest effect whatsoever.   I have had this most conclusively proved—at least, to my own satisfaction.

4

Stigand used a ·256. He was attacked unexpectedly one day by a cow. He blazed off in her face; but she took not the slightest notice of his little ·256. She got him down and proceeded to jab a tusk through his thigh, fortunately without damaging the femoral artery.

Palmer-Kerrison used a ·318. When on the Elephant Control staff in Uganda, on one occasion he ran into a troop of elephant which came for him at full speed. Whether they were charging or merely stampeding towards him, is neither here nor there. He was too close to avoid them, so fired at the nearest. But the bullet seemed to have no effect; and the nearest bull, the one at which he had fired, picked the wretched man up on one tusk and carried him like that for some distance before he eventually fell off—badly hurt in the stomach. The elephant, which had apparently been shot through the heart, carried on for some 100 yards or so and then fell dead.

I did not know either of these men personally; but the facts are well authenticated.

However, I did know four other men who were either killed or injured by elephant, through using rifles which lacked power. Of these : Two young fellows, one with a ·318 and the other with a ·333, stopped a night in my camp. They asked my opinion of their battery, stating that they had never seen an elephant outside of a zoo or a circus. My advice to them was, to return whence they came and swop both rifles for one more powerful weapon. But that they would not do. A few days later they, between them, succeeded in putting 42 shots into an elephant without bringing him down. He charged and killed one of the lads after seriously injuring the other—spine badly hurt, arm, leg and several ribs, broken. It seems that they were firing together each time they caught up with the elephant; eventually he ambushed them in a place wherein he had the advantage. When the elephant charged, one youngster, who was slightly in front of his companion, fired several shots into the elephant's head and chest ; but his light bullets were incapable of stopping or even turning the brute, who was now definitely out for blood. He grabbed the wretched lad in his trunk and hurled him savagely against a tree, in his stride, as it were, and without slowing in the slightest ; and continued his charge at the second youngster who was also blazing away at him now. He grabbed him also in his trunk, flung him high in the air, and then when he came down kicked him backwards and forwards between forefeet and hind feet as though playing with a football. Then, apparently feeling the effects of his own wounds, the elephant moved slowly away a short distance and leant up against a tree. He died there, still leaning against the tree in such a way that I was able to count the bullet wounds when, later, I arrived on the scene.

Another was a District Commissioner in Nyasaland. He swore by his ·350 magnum, with which he had shot several elephant. As is always the case when a couple of enthusiasts meet, we commenced discussing rifles and, in reply to a question, I told him that he was asking for trouble ; his little ·350 magnum was good enough for Jumbo in the open, but not in thick cover, and that John Rigby himself, who built the little rifle, would be the first to admit it.

" X ", as we may as well call him, laughed at my croaking ; but only four or five days later he followed a troop of elephant into a dense thicket of bush, shot the leader and was immediately attacked by an infuriated cow in a precisely similar manner to that which I have described. Although he blazed off in her face—as with Stigand's cow—she took not the slightest notice. With a blow of her trunk she knocked the man down, and then proceeded to kneel down, herself, beside him and endeavour to puncture him with her tusks. In this she failed ; but her rolled-up trunk smashed several ribs, and took most of the skin and flesh off one side of his face.

The fourth man whom I knew personally was a Russian

who swore by the ·423 (10·75 mm.).   Now in this case I
rather fancy that it was either the rifle or its ammunition
which let the man down, and not lack of power, because
he would persist in using cheap German rifles and invariably obtained his ammunition from the same source.

I was camped only a few miles away and his boys came
running in in a great state, one morning, to tell me that he
had been killed by an elephant.   Of course, I went along
with them ; but there was nothing to be done : He had,
quite literally, been wiped out of existence—just as a
native will wipe out, with a twist of his foot, the mark
where he has expectorated.   There was nothing to pick
up save his boots—with his feet still in them—his belt
and his hat ; he, himself, had been stamped and squashed
and trampled until there was nothing left but a stain on the
ground.

Numerous other incidents of a similar description could
be quoted ; but the foregoing are, I think, sufficiently
illuminating to uphold my contention that the light
bullet cannot be safely used against elephant other than
in the open.   If you are sufficiently interested in the
subject to look up records, you will find that in the vast
majority of cases where men are killed or injured by
elephant in Africa, that such men were either using rifles
throwing very light bullets or else cheap, mass-production
weapons which let them down at the critical moment.

I am not, of course, referring to the old black-powder
days, when misfires were the principal cause of fatalities ;
nor to those utterly inexperienced young beginners who,
having wounded an elephant, rush blindly after him
without waiting for their tracker and are killed by the
elephant, which has ambushed them, before they can fire
a shot at all.   Such men might as well have been armed
with walking sticks—or field guns—the result would have
been the same.

As I have already stated—but it will bear repetition—
the mere capacity to kill, *alone*, is not enough.   Before

a rifle can be termed a safe, suitable and satisfactory weapon for elephant, it must have sufficient power to be able to be absolutely relied upon to knock down an elephant under all conditions. " Shock ", as applied to heavy, massive-boned animals like elephant, does not refer to killing power, but to the ability of the rifle to knock the animal down. And this is where so many men go astray.

It is an astonishing thing to me that even Bell, probably the greatest exponent of the small-bore, should have so completely missed the point in this connection. In that excellent book of his, *The Wanderings of an Elephant Hunter*, he writes as follows :

> . . . I have never been able to appreciate " shock " as applied to killing game. It seems to me that you cannot hope to kill an elephant weighing six tons by " shock " unless you hit him with a field-gun. And yet nearly all writers advocate the use of large-bores as they " shock " the animal so much more than small bores. They undoubtedly " shock " the firer more, but I fail to see the difference they are going to make to the recipient of the bullet. If you expect to produce upon him by the use of large bores the effect a handful of shot had upon the Jumping Frog of Calaveras County, you will be disappointed. Wounded non-vitally he will go just as far and be just as savage with 500 grains of lead as with 200. And 100 grains in the right place are as good as ten million.

Now all this is perfectly true—every word of it. But the point is that nobody *does* expect to kill an elephant by " shock " !

Both barrels from a double ·600 in the belly will have little more apparent effect on him than a single shot from a ·275 (Bell's favourite rifle) in the same place. But the 900-grain bullet from the ·600-bore in the head, even if it missed the brain by a considerable amount, would knock the elephant down and out, right out—unconscious ; whereas the 173-grain bullet from the ·275-bore in the same place would do nothing of the sort. " Shock " as applied to elephant should, therefore, read " knock-out " blow.

And the reason why an elephant requires such a tremendously heavy blow to stun him is to be found in the fact that the bones which comprise his skull are not solid, as they are in other animals, but on the contrary are comprised of a vast number of air-cells. Consequently, instead of the blow being transmitted directly to the brain, as it would be in other game, it is, to a very great extent, absorbed by these air-cells which act as shock-absorbers. And so it is that, to bring about the desired effect, the bullet must either strike very close to the brain indeed, or else a tremendously heavy blow must be inflicted. And a small, light bullet obviously cannot inflict a tremendously heavy blow, no matter at what speed it is travelling.

I have stood beside a man and watched him put 5 shots from a ·425-bore magazine rifle into an elephant's head without, apparently, having the slightest effect on the animal. The elephant, a fine tusker, was standing broadside on to us at a range of about 30–35 paces ; his head exposed, but his body concealed by a large baobab tree. It was the first wild elephant that my companion had ever seen. I told him where to place his bullet ; but in his excitement he fired too high and too far forward. I heard the smack of the bullet and saw a little spurt of dust fly off the elephant's head (he had been plastering himself with mud which had dried in the sun). The bull stampeded directly across our front ; and my companion ripped off the contents of his magazine at him. I distinctly heard all four succeeding shots hit, and saw the little dust-puffs fly up. But that elephant took not the slightest notice. It was only when I realized that my companion's magazine was empty and that the elephant was getting away, that I swung up my own rifle—a Holland double ·465 " Royal "—and brought the animal down.

If somebody threw a cricket ball at you and hit you between the eyes it would, in all probability, knock you down ; but if they threw a ping-pong ball at you, even using a catapult with which to obtain velocity, and hit you in the same place, it is extremely improbable that it would fell you.

The only explanation that there can be of Bell's success with his ·275 may be summed up in the one word " Luck ". In view of the facts, there can be no other explanation. It was just his luck not to be attacked when in such a position that he could not extricate himself by some means or another, apart from knocking down the elephant.

There is another grave disadvantage of ultra small-bore bullets. That is, that they cannot always be relied upon to kill cleanly and instantaneously although they may seem to be perfectly placed. Sutherland states that on two or three occasions he pierced the brain of a large elephant—as he found on subsequent examination— with small-bore bullets without killing the animals, and was obliged to finish them off later. Selous in one of his books describes how he examined the heart of an elephant through which he had fired three bullets before the animal fell.

To which can be added the additional fact that practically all the most successful and most experienced professional elephant hunters, both of the past and of the present day, used and use rifles throwing bullets of not less than 400 grains for use in thick cover.

Neuman and Selous shot by far the greater number of their elephant in the days of black powder when large bores were essential. But to take the most experienced hunters of more recent times :

Sutherland was probably the first man to reach four figures ; he used a pair of double ·577's.

Pearson, who had also killed 1,000 elephant, in the days when he did most of his hunting used a similar battery ; though after joining the Elephant Control staff in Uganda he became a convert to, and staunch upholder of, the magazine rifle, provided it threw a sufficiently heavy bullet (not under 400 grains).

Banks of Uganda, probably the most experienced elephant hunter in Africa at the present day, killed his thousandth elephant some considerable time ago. He uses a double throwing a bullet of not less than 480 grains in thick cover, and a medium-bore magazine in the open.

Pitman, Game Warden of Uganda, uses a double ·450.

Blaney Percival of Kenya used a double ·450.

Ritchie of Kenya used a double ·470.

Anderson of Kenya used a double ·577.

Hunter of Kenya uses a double ·577.

Teare, Game Warden of Tanganyika, uses a ·404.

Of the Game Rangers of Tanganyika, one swears by a double ·470; another by a double ·465; yet a third by a double ·400; whilst two others are quite content with ·404's.

In Kenya generally, doubles in the ·450–·470-bore group are the favourites for use in thick cover; with medium-bore high-velocity magazines for use in the open.

Fairweather of Tanganyika used a double ·450 No. 2.

Blunt of Tanganyika always swore by the ·416.

In the Belgian Congo, doubles ranging upwards from ·450 are the most widely used.

Here in Portuguese East, doubles ranging from ·450 up are generally preferred for thick cover; though many men use large medium-bore magazine rifles. But that, I think, is principally because they cannot afford doubles.

All of which is, surely, sufficiently conclusive proof that the small-bore and the light bullet are definitely unsuitable for elephant.

There are, at the present time, a score or more of excellent rifles on the market all of which are eminently suitable for elephant hunting. It is only men who have shot their first few elephant with black-powder weapons that are really in a position to appreciate thoroughly the phenomenal power of the modern Nitro-Express rifle. I killed my first elephant with a short sporting Martini-Henry (·577/·450) ; black powder and a lead bullet. (Banks of Uganda tells me that, curiously enough, he also killed his first elephant with a similar weapon.) Since then I have used practically everything on the market from ·275 to ·600, both inclusive.

As I have stated in a preceding chapter, the " Knock-Out " values which I give in the right-hand column of the ballistic tables approximate to an altogether remarkable degree with my actual experience of the rifles under practical conditions of sport. And in my experience, 50 knock-out values are the very minimum number which ought ever to be used by a beginner, and the more the better (a point or two either way, of course, makes no difference for all practical purposes). Any rifle (with one exception, which I shall discuss presently) which shows a K-O value of not less than 50 can safely be relied upon to knock down an elephant in any circumstances, though it may not stun him. Over 60 values are necessary if he is to be stunned and not merely temporarily dazed— assuming that the brain is missed by an appreciable amount.

That one exception that I mentioned is the ·440 (11·2 mm.). This rifle is not a satisfactory weapon for elephant owing to the very poor weight to diameter ratio of the bullet. The bullet is light but of large diameter and fairly high velocity ; the disadvantage of this combination is that the bullet on encountering a massive bone, has not got sufficient weight—that is, it is not sufficiently massive—to enable it to overcome the tremendous resistance which it encounters owing to its large diameter. And the result, far more often than not, is that the bullet tends to blow to pieces before it can find its way into a vital spot. At the same time, it *could* be taken with a reasonable degree of safety, though not of satisfaction, against elephant.

A thoroughly experienced hunter, who knows for an absolute, positive fact that his nerve will not fail him in a tight corner, may use a slightly less powerful rifle ; but I am convinced that 40 values are the absolute minimum amount that should ever be taken against elephant in thick cover by anybody. 40 values can be relied upon to turn an elephant ; and will usually knock him down if you slam them into his head.

In other words, it can be definitely stated that there is no less-powerful rifle on the market at the present time than Holland's ·375 magnum, which ought ever to be taken against elephant in thick cover. And even there you are running pretty close to the margin of safety—too close, in my opinion, for any but an experienced man. Of course, for the licensee in British Africa who can only obtain permission to shoot two, or at the most three, elephant a year a rifle such as a Holland ·375 magnum is a perfectly safe weapon, since he will be hunting elephant so seldom that in all probability he will hunt for years without being attacked ; in addition, since he will have been using the rifle on all other kinds of game all the time, he will be thoroughly accustomed to it and so will be able to use it with vastly greater precision than he would a much heavier and more powerful weapon that he seldom fired. I, myself, have shot scores of elephant with this rifle and have never had an anxious moment ; not even when surrounded by a large herd. It has never let me down yet, and I see no reason to suppose that it ever will.

But I most certainly do not recommend, in any circumstances—other, of course, than shooting in the open—any less-powerful weapon than Holland's ·375 magnum.

With regard to the question of double or magazine : In elephant hunting it is really a matter of **personal** preference.   Granted that the bullet is sufficiently heavy, either can be used with complete safety and satisfaction. There are, of course, occasions when one or other would be definitely preferable ; consequently, the ideal battery should include both, particularly in the case of the professional or would-be-professional hunter.

There are several arguments in favour of the double for use in thick cover : In the first place, there is the question of general handiness due to its shortness, compactness and perfect balance.   Then there is the question of silence. Now if you have caught up with your elephant somewhere round about midday, when the sun is warm, you will often find that they have spread out a little and are dozing and sleeping in the shade.   If you drop one, say the leader, with a clean brain shot the others, more often than not, will stand there, ears out and trunks up, unable to place the danger zone and consequently unable to make up their minds as to the best line for the stampede. Because in dense bush or heavy forest it is frequently extremely difficult to decide just from whence a shot has come.   The unavoidable clatter when the bolt is manipulated during the reloading process with a magazine rifle will inevitably discover your position to the herd. Even the sharp, metallic " click " of the ejectors in an ejector double rifle will all too frequently be sufficient to lose you a second shot.   Because in very thick cover, unless you know for an absolute positive fact that each and every member of the herd is in front of you, you must never fire the left barrel until you have reloaded the right. It is absolutely imperative that it should be kept in reserve in case of a sudden, unexpected attack from very close quarters.

But with a non-ejector, with a little care, there need not be a sound of any sort whilst you reload the barrel which you have fired.   There is no sound as you open the breech and quietly remove the fired cartridge ; slip it into an empty pocket or down the front of your shirt—

anywhere at all so that it does not make a noise ; slip another cartridge quietly into the chamber ; and then, holding the top lever open with your thumb, quietly close the breech and let the lever come slowly back into position.   Then, with both barrels once more fully loaded you can move quietly round amongst the herd until you spot another good tusker.   You drop him, and still have your second barrel in immediate reserve in case of a sudden attack.

With every ejector double rifle that I have had in the past, I have had to remove the ejector springs and use it as a non-ejector because of that click as the breech is broken.   Further, if the springs are very powerful, the empty shell will frequently ring as it is thrown clear of the breech ; besides which there is always the possibility of it striking against your chest or shoulder and falling down with a clatter against the butt of the rifle ; and even if that does not happen, then it is certain to fall on the only stone within a radius of a hundred square miles. But easily worst of all is the loud " clang " with which the breech closes ; and you cannot avoid it, because the closing of the breech has to recock the ejectors.   Any metallic sound of any sort or description whatsoever is, naturally, quite foreign to the Bush, and therefore spells danger to the herd.

For elephant I very much prefer a non-ejector, though admittedly there are occasions when ejectors are an asset. Still, in my experience, such occasions are mighty few and far between and are far more than offset by the vastly greater number of occasions when they are an infernal nuisance.   Accordingly, being a very poor man, I have my doubles built as non-ejectors, as I can see no fun in paying an additional ten guineas for ejectors which I should not be using.

There are, and always will be, two schools of thought : Those who prefer doubles and those who prefer magazines. Personally I very much prefer the double, particularly in thick cover ; and I am inclined to think that the great majority of the magazine school is composed of men who either have never used a double, or else have only used an inferior-quality weapon.   I have never come across a man who had used a really perfectly-fitting and perfectly-balanced best-quality double who would willingly discard it in favour of a magazine.

The only disadvantage of the double is the cost, and this is certainly serious.   But second-hand best-quality weapons can usually be obtained at considerably reduced prices, and if they are bought from their original makers they are guaranteed to be in sound, serviceable condition and can, therefore, be absolutely relied upon.   A good second-hand best-quality rifle is a vastly better pro-position than a new cheaper-quality weapon at the same figure ; though a second-quality rifle from any one of the best makers is a thoroughly sound, reliable weapon, the accuracy of which may be depended upon.

Commander D. E. Blunt relates a story concerning that well-known amateur hunter, the late Sir Alfred Sharpe.   He writes :

> . . . He has had some miraculous escapes, two of which he reckons were due to using a double barrel instead of a magazine rifle.   On one occasion he was hunting in open country without any kind of cover and grass knee-high, when an elephant charged him.   Having fired his two rounds and accounted for his beast, he was attacked by another. As the boy carrying his ammunition had bolted, and as there were no trees to climb, he went to ground, lying down and watching the elephant as it came towards him.

Now how could any man, finding himself in a pre-dicament of that description, honestly blame it on his rifle?   When all is said and done, the finest double rifle that had ever been built cannot reasonably be expected to fire more than two rounds without being reloaded ! In a case of that sort, I say that if there is any blame floating around it must come home to roost on the sportsman's own shoulders for tackling more than one

elephant with a double rifle and not having a single
solitary spare round of ammunition on him.   Granted
that wealthy sportsmen are not accustomed to, and do not
usually care about, carrying any unnecessary weights ;
but surely two spare cartridges, or even only one, in
the breast pocket of your shirt cannot be termed a
tremendous load.

Personally, when tackling more than one elephant
with a double rifle, I invariably slip two cartridges between the fingers of my left hand.   In that way they do
not interfere in the slightest with your handling of the
rifle, yet are immediately convenient for reloading and
save you having to fumble for them.   With all due respect
to the late Sir Alfred, I consider that that was a very
unfair and extremely ill-advised remark to have made.
And I feel sure that Sir Alfred on due reflection would,
himself, have been the first to admit it.   Because many
a young sportsman, contemplating his first battery and
feeling attracted to a double, on hearing or reading of
a sportsman of Sir Alfred's undoubted experience making
a statement of that description might not unreasonably
be tempted to shy like frightened colts from the double
and invest in a magazine rifle ;   a type of weapon in which
they might not, perhaps, have the same instinctive
confidence which they felt that they would have had
in the double.

And when tackling dangerous game at close quarters,
it is imperative that the sportsman should have absolute
confidence in whatever weapon he is handling.

But if you use a magazine rifle in thick cover, on no
account should the barrel be more than 24 inches in
length.   In dense, matted tangles of bush every unnecessary inch on the length of the rifle counts heavily
against it.   The longer the rifle the greater possibility
there is of the barrel catching in a trailing vine, creeper,
branch, overhang of a bush or something of the sort, should
it be necessary to swing round quickly for a shot in an

unexpected direction. Remember, the long bolt action of a magazine rifle will in any case add considerably to the total length of the weapon. When the very short ranges at which elephant are shot is borne in mind, there cannot be the slightest necessity for barrels of more than 24 inches in length on any rifle, double, single or magazine.

The " Old Timer's " maxim holds as good today as it did in the days of black powder : " Git as close as y' can, laddie—an' then *git ten yards closer*."

In thick cover, 20 paces may be considered as a very long shot ; anywhere else, upwards of 40 paces is long-range shooting at elephant. Now if a rifle fitted with a 28-inch barrel will kill an elephant at 50 yards range, it will kill him just as effectively with a 24-inch barrel and be an infinitely handier and better-balanced weapon into the bargain. A double could be fitted with longer barrels and still remain a much better-balanced weapon owing to the greater concentration of weight between the hands that there is with this design. But even with a double, there is no reason whatever why the barrels need be more than 24 inches in length. Experience has shown that 24-inch barrels will shoot as accurately as can ever be needed in practical sport. Theoretically, perhaps, the longer the barrel the more accurate the rifle and doubtless if you were shooting at some fantastic range like 1,000 yards that would be true in actual fact ; in practical sport, however, there are grave disadvantages in too long a barrel : the longer the barrel the more pronounced the flip, and this is a point that assumes considerable importance in the hinterland of Africa where the temperature varies to the extent that it does between daybreak and midday. In addition to which, a very long barrel can be a positive danger in thick cover if you are called upon to swing round quickly for a shot in an unexpected direction. I knew a man who was very nearly killed by a buffalo he had wounded and was following up : feeling sure that the beast was in a thicket of bush on his half-left front, he did not take sufficient notice of a clump of long grass on his half-right. Just as he passed the grass, the buffalo charged ; and in swinging round to face the charge, the muzzle of the man's rifle—a ·425 magazine with a ridiculous 28-inch barrel sticking out beyond the long bolt action—caught in something and he only just managed to free it in time ; even as it was the buffalo's forehead practically touched the muzzle as the hunter fired.

In view of the very short ranges at which elephant are shot, there can be no earthly necessity for long barrels. My first doubles were fitted with 28-inch barrels and I found them very satisfactory ; I then came down to 26-inch barrels and found them infinitely better. After that I started using 24-inch and 25-inch barrels and swore by them. Nowadays I would not dream of having a double or single built for me with longer barrels than 26 inches ; the 27-inch and 28-inch barrelled weapons actually seem clumsy and ungainly to me now. Further, although on paper there must be a slight falling off in velocity and therefore in power when the barrel-length is reduced, as far as all practical sport is concerned I can definitely state that I have not noticed the slightest difference in the killing power of the rifles ; and in several of them I have used the same cartridges in three and even four different lengths of barrel.

The shorter the barrels the handier the rifle and the more perfectly and more easily can it be balanced, because of the greater concentration of weight between the hands. Balance, to my mind, is every bit as important as accuracy ; because no matter how accurate your rifle may be, if it is not properly balanced an accurate snap-shot is an utter impossibility. I remember I had this most forcibly brought home to me once, many years ago, when I was carrying an old double-hammer ·450 No. 2, 28-inch barrels and a very short stock. It was a ghastly thing, no attempt at balancing it ever having been made. On swinging the butt up to my shoulder I had to, quite literally, heave the muzzles up with my left hand to get the sights in line. I was very badly off for fresh meat one day so, on encountering a.troop of zebra at a range of 25 paces or so, swung up the rifle for a quick snap-shot at the stallion. At the shot he lurched and bounded away ; only to pull up again 10 or 15 paces farther along. I again swung the rifle up and took another quick shot at him ; only to have the same thing happen once more. It was only now, when I came to reload, that I remembered that it was this brute of a weapon that I was using. The third shot was centrally placed. On examining the zebra, I found that the first shot had blown his near fore hoof off ! And the second had smashed his leg, the same one, just below the knee !

When shooting with a perfectly-fitting, perfectly-balanced double rifle at close ranges it is not necessary to think about the sights at all : Just look at the spot on the animal in which you wish to place your bullet, swing the rifle up, and press the trigger as the butt settles into your shoulder. It is an incalculable asset when tackling elephant (or any large beasts, for that matter) at close quarters ; particularly will you find it so if you do any work amongst marauding elephant at night.

Since cordite superseded black powder the only rifles really which have been dignified by the name of " Elephant Rifles " are the ·577- and ·600-bores. Principally, I suppose, because such weapons would be used against elephant, and elephant only.

The ·600-bore is, of course, the most powerful rifle that has ever been built ; but it is rarely used nowadays, as it is generally considered that the tremendous power is more than offset by the weight which is such that the average man might find difficulty in handling the rifle quickly in an emergency, particularly if he happened to be fatigued.

I have frequently heard men say that the bullet for

5

the ·600 is too heavy for the powder charge. Now on being interpreted, this can only mean one of two things —or both of them—i.e. that the trajectory is not sufficiently flat ; and that the bullet lacks penetration. Well, all I can say to that is that such men clearly show that they have never used a ·600, or they would not be guilty of making such a remark. In view of the very close ranges at which elephant are shot, the ·600 has as flat a trajectory as could ever be needed ; whilst as for penetration, no man in his right mind could ask for anything better. I killed a considerable number of elephant some years ago with a little 24-inch barrelled double ·600 by Jeffery of London.

I remember shooting a large bull at a range of about 35 paces—frontal brain shot. As I had had an argument with a man over this question of penetration, I broke off a young bamboo shoot and pushed it into the wound as far as it would go. Then, grasping it with my thumb against the elephant's forehead, I withdrew the bamboo and measured it against the barrels of my rifle (I had no tape with me). It was at least 3 inches longer than the barrels.

However, it is generally conceded nowadays that the additional power of these rifles, with the inevitable concomitant of additional weight, is not necessary. The majority of men considering that a theoretical mathematical muzzle energy in the neighbourhood of 5,000 ft.-lb., or thereabouts, is ample for the heaviest game. And for the non-professional sportsman I should be inclined to agree. At the same time, it is only fair to the ·577- and ·600-bore rifles to mention a point tremendously in their favour ; it is this : In dense bush it is all too frequently impossible to do anything but knock the elephant down on a head shot which you know cannot possibly find the brain, and then tear your way through the bush in the hope that you will be in time to finish him off before he gathers wits together sufficiently to do anything about it. Obviously, the heavier the blow you hit him the better your chance of bagging him. As I have already pointed out, over 60 Knock-Out values are necessary to stun an elephant ; accordingly, from this it will be seen that it is no use attempting this game with any less-powerful weapon than a ·450. Rifles in the ·450-·470 group will stun an elephant for anything up to 5 minutes or so, depending on how close to the brain you hit him ; the ·500's may keep him down for anything up to 10 minutes ; the ·577 will knock him out for possibly 20 minutes ; and the ·600 for anything up to half an hour. (I am, of course, considering only the full load and not reduced loads.) So that from this it will be seen that if you are armed with a ·577 or ·600 you will have ample time in which to bag perhaps two, three, or even more, of the first elephant's companions before bothering about him, if they are in no hurry to depart. I do not consider that the professional elephant hunter is properly armed unless his battery includes either a ·577- or ·600-bore.

The ·450 is probably the most popular bore that has ever been introduced. The various rifles in the ·470-bore group were only brought in when the importation of the ·450 into India and the Sudan was prohibited. Although on paper there is a small difference between them all, as far as practical sport is concerned there is nothing whatever to choose between any of them from the point of view of killing power. The ·450 No. 2, ·465 and ·470, however, have the very decided advantage of an appreciably lower chamber pressure.

I have killed more elephant with the ·450 No. 2 and ·465-bores than with all my other rifles put together. They will, either of them, satisfactorily answer any questions that you could ever wish to ask them. If I had to choose between them I should probably decide on the ·465 ; but that is only because it is a Holland speciality, and because Messrs. Holland & Holland build their ·465 to average a pound lighter than similar

rifles built by their contemporaries.   Now that extra pound
in weight is nothing, less than nothing, when you are
handling a rifle in your gunsmith's showrooms ; but it
is quite another matter when you have been carrying it
for hours at a stretch under impossibly difficult conditions
in the sweltering heat.   Admittedly, 11¼ lb., the average
weight of rifles in this group, cannot by any stretch of
the imagination be termed excessively heavy ; but why,
when they so obviously *can* be built to weigh but 10¼ lbs.,
carry that extra pound weight round with you ?

For the sportsman who prefers a magazine rifle at all
times and who does a considerable amount of elephant
hunting, Gibbs' ·505-bore Mauser is a splendid weapon.
It is very moderately priced ; it is a tremendously
powerful weapon ; and as I know from using one in the
past, has no unpleasant recoil though it weighs but
10½ lb. or a trifle over.   I have also used Jeffery's ·500-
bore Mauser, and exactly the same remarks apply to it ;
but I would never recommend it because as far as I know
the ammunition is only obtainable from Germany.

Blunt, a staunch upholder of the magazine rifle, always
swore by his Rigby ·416.   D. D. Lyell, another magazine
enthusiast, used and recommends a Jeffery ·404.   The
·404 has proved itself over and over again as being an
eminently safe, sound and suitable weapon for elephant.
The fact that the highly efficient and exhaustively trained
Native hunters employed by the Governments of Uganda
and Tanganyika for elephant control and cultivation protection are all armed with ·404's speaks, I think, for itself.

A number of men, particularly of the older generation
of elephant hunters, recommend a pair of rifles.   Now
I, most emphatically, do not agree with this advice.   In
the first place, you may or may not have time in which
to change rifles if you are suddenly and unexpectedly
attacked from close quarters. Palmer-Kerrison of
Uganda, whose misadventure I have already related, had
a heavier weapon with which to back up his ·318 ; but

on the occasion on which he was injured, he had no time in which to take it over. Admittedly, had he had a pair of large bores he would in all probability have been able to stop the charge. But in very thick cover, if you fire both barrels of the rifle in your hands, it is by no means easy or pleasant to have to turn round to exchange rifles with your gun-bearer, perhaps only to find that he has bolted. Because, although many lads can be absolutely relied upon to stand by you, your regular gun-bearer will occasionally want a spot of leave or be sick or something, and then, having been dependent upon him for so long, you will be apt to feel a trifle lost without him. Of course, the professional hunter will almost certainly have at least two reliable gun-bearers ; but naturally I am writing this principally for the benefit of beginners. Nor, if you have learnt to depend on a second rifle, can you possibly be so confident when you have to rely upon only the one.

It is imperative that the hunter should learn to rely, absolutely, upon himself and the rifle in his hands.

Bluff-nosed solid bullets are the only kind that should ever be used against elephant. Solid, pointed bullets are not reliable owing to their tendency to glance and turn over on entering, particularly if they happen to encounter a bone. Expanding bullets are not satisfactory and should never be used, other than in the case of the ·577- and ·600-bores, and then only for heart or lung shots.

To sum up, then :

The ideal battery for elephant hunting consists of a non-ejector double rifle throwing a ·480- or 500-grain bullet for use in thick cover, with or without a high-velocity medium- or large-medium-bore magazine rifle for use in the open. (The professional should also have a double ·577- or ·600-bore.)

If, however, you prefer a magazine rifle at all times, it can be used with perfect satisfaction and safety provided that it throws a bullet of not less than 400 grains.

CHAPTER IV

Rifles for Rhino Hunting

THE rhino that inhabit the great open plains of British East Africa are easy money. Provided the wind is right, all that you have to do is walk up and shoot. Any modern rifle firing bluff-nosed, solid, metal-covered bullets will suffice. But the rhino that live in the dense bush zones of Central and South-East Central Africa are a very different proposition. They choose the most impenetrable tangles of thorn bush, and I have seen them go through stuff, that even a stampeding elephant wouldn't face, at full speed as though it was paper.

Rhino are apt to be an infernal nuisance to the elephant hunter. Time and again have I been charged by rhino when following up a troop or herd of elephant. In not-too-thick scrub or open forest you can generally manage to dodge the brute, when he will usually just continue at full speed in the direction in which he was facing. But in thick thorn-bush, particularly if it is of the hawk's-bill thorn variety, it is frequently a physical impossibility to dodge. You must just stand your ground and shoot the brute—which means goodbye to any chance that you may have had with the elephant. Under these circumstances rhino are looked upon much as are pike in a trout stream.

But if you are actually hunting him he ceases to be vermin and, like the pike in an Irish lough, instantly becomes a fine sporting antagonist. But rhino hunting in thick bush is a game that one very rarely sees being played. And really it is rather extraordinary, because it is an intensely exciting sport; the excitement commencing the moment you leave camp, and continuing uninterruptedly until you return again. (I am, of course, assuming a district in which rhino are numerous.) You never know when you are going to encounter one of the brutes : you may tramp for hours without seeing one ; you may find yourself being attacked within a few minutes of leaving camp. Of course, by no means all rhino will attack ; but since you never know when you are going to meet the bad-tempered one, it is merely common sense to go about the business as though they were all the same.

In the dense, matted tangles of bush beloved by the rhino visibility is usually limited to a matter of feet ; 25 yards is a very long shot. The range will usually be found to work out at from 2 or 3 feet to 10 or 12 paces. In other words, since you are so very close to the beasts if you *do* happen to encounter them, the chances are at least even as to whether he comes or not. But the point is that since, if he does come, he will be coming from such very close quarters and will arrive so shortly after his first snort of warning, that it behoves you to be very much on the alert and *carrying your own rifle*. The pluckiest and most willing of gunbearers cannot be blamed if he jumps for his life when he sees a rhino's horn coming straight for his midriff and only perhaps 2 or 3 feet away. It is not fair on the lad to expect him to do anything else.

And with regard to the most suitable rifles for this sport, the first question that crops up is : double or magazine ? Now here there can be no two opinions— no two possible opinions : a double rifle is out and away the best type of weapon ; in fact, if the bush is very dense and the rhino numerous, then a double is not merely preferable, but definitely essential. And there are several reasons for this :

First : In very dense bush every unnecessary inch on the length of the rifle counts heavily against it ; particularly when you may, and probably will, have to swing round suddenly. A double is much shorter and more compact than the magazine.

Second : As I have already mentioned elsewhere, balance helps one enormously to swing and mount a rifle or gun for a quick and accurate snap-shot. No magazine can possibly be as well balanced as an equally good double, owing to the greater concentration of weight that there is between the hands with the latter type. No matter how accurate your rifle may be, if it is not properly balanced a quick and *accurate* snap-shot is an utter impossibility other than by a fluke—and you cannot afford to rely upon flukes when tackling dangerous game at close quarters.

Third : And this is very nearly as important—the rapidity with which the first shot can be fired from a double.

All powerful magazine rifles are fitted with a Mauser pattern bolt action in which the safety catch has to be twisted across from one side to the other before the rifle is ready for action. This operation takes an appreciable time and cannot possibly be performed whilst the rifle is on its way up to the shoulder. Accordingly, an appreciable time must elapse before you can get off your first shot. On the other hand, the safety slide on a double can be snicked forward whilst the rifle is actually being swung to the shoulder and mounted for the shot. There is not an instant's unnecessary delay. Of course, if you are following up a wounded animal, you will carry your rifle " at the ready " with the safety in the firing position, irrespective of the type of weapon. But you cannot walk about in the thick bush all day carrying a heavy rifle in that manner when you are just hunting and waiting for something to turn up.

Now with regard to the choice of bore. Where the knocking down of a heavy and dangerous animal at very close quarters is concerned, bullet weight is of primary importance. Within reasonable limits, a small, heavy bullet will inflict a heavier blow than a larger diametered bullet of lighter weight. (An excellent example of this is to be found in the case of the standard 400-grain bullet for the ·450/·400 or ·404 and the 347-grain bullet for the ·423 (10·75 mm.) Mauser. The former hits the heavier blow of the two, although it is of smaller calibre.) My Knock-Out values clearly show this ; and my own practical experience fully corroborates. Generally speaking, however, it may be taken as a rough rule that the larger the bullet, the heavier it is, and, therefore, the heavier the blow it delivers. At the same time, it should be borne in mind that there are exceptions. I do not know what a rhino weighs, but it is probably somewhere in the vicinity of from 2 to 3 tons. And 2 or 3 tons of bad temper coming from 20 to 25 miles an hour takes a deal of stopping ! I should certainly not recommend a bullet of less than 400 grains in weight, and personally I prefer the 480- and 500-grain bullets. (A Holland ·375 magnum loaded with 300-grain solids can be used, though even here you are running pretty close to the margin of safety. I mention it separately because there are several other rifles throwing bullets of round about 300 grains which are definitely not powerful enough.)

Of course, the smallest rifle used in the African bush, the ·256 (6·5 mm.), when loaded with bluff-nosed solids, is capable of killing the largest rhino, or elephant for that matter, in all Africa—provided that rhino or elephant is sufficiently obliging to expose a vital spot. But that is a very different thing to stopping a charge at a range of only a few feet when it may be a physical impossibility to place your bullet in the brain. A knock-down blow is essential—absolutely essential—and only a heavy bullet can definitely be relied upon to inflict it.

Although there is a slight difference between them all on paper, for all practical purposes of sport there is nothing whatever to choose between the various cartridges in the ·450–·470-bore group, save only on

the question of chamber-pressure. On this score the
·450 No. 2, ·465 and ·470 have the advantage.

Ejectors are not necessary for rhino.

Solid, pointed bullets should never be used on any
kind of game. Bluff-nosed solids are the only satisfactory
kind. Expanding bullets can be used for body shots at
rhino, provided they are sufficiently heavy. For anything under 400 grains, solids should be used. With
bullets ranging between 400 and 570 grains, solids should
be used for head shots and raking shots ; and soft-nosed
bullets with the lead barely showing at the nose for body
shots. If too much lead is exposed the lighter bullets in
this group may pack up too soon. Westley Richards'
round-capped bullet—*not* the " L.T." capped—is very
effective for this work, as it is specially designed for
expansion combined with penetration, whereas the
" L.T." pattern is intended for rapid expansion. For
bullets heavier than ·570 grains—there are only two rifles
throwing heavier bullets : the ·577- and ·600-bores—
plain soft-nosed bullets with plenty of lead showing at
the nose are wonderfully deadly for body shots, with
soft-nosed bullets having the lead just showing for head
and raking shots. Here again, the Westley Richards's
capped bullet for the ·577 (not obtainable for the ·600)
is excellent.

To sum up, then :

The ideal battery for rhino hunting in thick bush
consists of a double rifle throwing a bullet of not less
than 400 grains, and preferably 480 or 500 grains. In
open country any modern rifle firing bluff-nosed bullets
will do.

CHAPTER V

Rifles for Hippo Hunting

THE usual method of shooting hippo—just potting at their heads in the water—is rather a miserable business when viewed as a sport ; though it is sometimes necessary to thin out their numbers on account of the immense amount of damage they do. For this purpose any rifle you prefer will do provided it shoots bluff-nosed solid bullets. In districts in which they have been shot up to any considerable extent, however, hippo are extremely chary about showing themselves in daylight ; so that some other means has to be devised for getting in touch with them. One method is to search along the river bank or marge of the lake until you find the place where they come ashore ; then, just as it grows dark, take up your position on the down-wind side of their path and wait for them to come up out of the water. Another method which provides not a little excitement and sometimes a measure of risk, is to either ambush them or hunt for them on their feeding-grounds, which may be miles away from the water ; it is amazing how far they will travel overland at night to get to some wretched native's food crops. The risk in this form of hunting is that there may be, and probably are, a number of hippo wandering about, but you have not the slightest idea as to where they all are. On the heels of the shot that you fire at one, the remainder will make a wild dash for the water, wherever it may be, since that spells safety for them. If there is no convenient and friendly tree behind which you can shelter, then your best plan is to rush up to the carcase of the hippo you have dropped and either stand or crouch behind it. You also have a fair chance of bumping into either elephant or rhino, or both, on your way to the hippo's feeding-grounds or when returning therefrom ; to say nothing of the possibility of stubbing your toe against a lion.

If you are trying to wipe out a " rogue " hippo—one that has developed a habit of charging and upsetting native dug-out canoes—and are paddling about in one of these crazy, cranky and unwieldy affairs shaped, possibly, not unlike a banana and leaking like a basket, in the hope of tempting the " rogue " to charge you and so give you a shot at hi n, you are likely to get all the excitement that any sane and sober man could want, particularly when you see several large crocs nosing round in the immediate vicinity.

For any of these forms of hunting the more powerful the rifle is the better ; weight does not matter because you are not carrying it for hours on end in the sweltering heat.   I would always recommend a double in preference to a magazine because of its infinitely better balance ; failing a double, I, personally, would prefer a powerful single-loader to any magazine.

If you are shooting hippo on land, load an expanding bullet in one barrel for broadside shots, and a solid in the other for head or neck shots.   For hippo in the water, solids only should be used.   For calibres ranging between ·400 and ·500 the lead should be just showing at the nose for body shots ; for ·577- and ·600-bores there should be plenty of lead exposed.

To sum up :

The best weapon for hippo hunting ashore is a powerful double—not less than ·400-bore ; and a similar weapon when hunting in a canoe.   If you are on shore and are shooting hippo in the water, any modern rifle firing bluff-nosed solid bullets will be perfectly satisfactory.

CHAPTER VI

Rifles for Buffalo Hunting

WHEN I speak of buffalo I am, of course, referring to the big Cape buffalo, as he is known, and which is invariably called to mind when buffalo are mentioned. Though in very great measure what I have to say with regard to rifles for buffalo hunting can be applied equally to rifles for the little forest buffalo of the Ituri Forest system, in the Belgian Congo, and over towards West Africa. Because, although he is considerably smaller than the big Cape buffalo and has not that massive, bullet-prouf boss of horn over his forehead, he is seldom found other than in the very densest cover and is well-known for his courage and ferocity when roused.

The African buffalo, then, save in exceptional circumstances has no wish to try conclusions with man and, prior to being wounded, will invariably clear off on winding or sighting him. I have it on good authority that buffalo suffering from rinderpest are apt to turn vicious and attack man without provocation ; and I know that if a herd is continually being shot up and its members constantly wounded and not killed, the entire herd is liable to turn man-killer and run down and trample and gore anybody at all, including women and children collecting firewood and wild fruit. There used to be a bad herd in Kenya years ago—and may still be, for all I know—though I do not know whether rinderpest or shooting was responsible ; there was another in the Luangwa Valley, in Northern Rhodesia, and there is no doubt that shooting was responsible there ; and a couple in the lower Zambezi Valley in Portuguese territory, which I know for a fact were driven frantic by the ghastly exhibitions of shooting to which they were subjected (by half-castes and South African Dutchmen in particular.)

These are the " exceptional circumstances " to which I have referred above. If buffalo are encountered in the open, any modern rifle firing bluff-nosed solid bullets will kill. But buffalo very much prefer long grass and thick scrub and bush. About the only time you can confidently expect to find them in the open is when the grass has been burnt off a large plain favoured by them. This plain must have water and mud-baths on it somewhere. If you get them out there you can certainly shoot them with a small-bore rifle ; though I do not recommend it. The reason is, that if you are tackling a large herd of buffalo out in the open without any sort of cover, you are apt to get a bad scare if you are not accustomed to the game and that is not going to steady you ; the result will probably be a wounded beast to follow up. Because if buffalo out in the open see you walking towards them, just like cattle in a large paddock that do not often see man, they will come jostling each other towards you. The pressure of those behind trying to get to the front to see you, will start the front line trotting and then the lot will break into a lumbering gallop. If there are several hundred in the herd, as there may well be, it is somewhat alarming to see this dense black mass coming thundering down on you : the pounding of hooves ; the rattling and clashing of mighty horns ; the clouds of dust and ashes of burnt grass thrown up in a great black pall. They will usually start coming when you are about 150 yards away. When they have covered about half the distance between you, they will usually pull up and have another look ; two or three of the biggest bulls, the leaders of the herd, will then come perhaps 10 yards or so closer and paw the ground till the dust flies, toss their great heads and snort, taking an occasional step or two towards you. This is just bluff, of course ; but if you are new to the game your nerve might easily fail when they again advance. If it does, and you turn to run, you stand a mighty good chance of being run down; but if your heart is in the right place you have nothing to worry about. Stand your ground and all will be well. The experienced man will let them come on until they are within 40 or 50 yards, when they will probably pull up again of their own accord. If they do not, then he just shouts; that will certainly stop them, and now is the time to open fire. At least two of the biggest bulls will be in front, only 40 or 50 yards away and no cover at all in between you; their heads will come up as they halt, their noses pointed towards you. Let one big fellow have it squarely in the chest; and then, as the second wheels round to go and exposes his broadside, give him the left barrel through the shoulder.

As I have already hinted, if this is your first experience of this nature, you may not be too steady when it comes to shooting—it gives even an old hand a bit of a thrill still!—and unsteadiness, even at 50 yards, can easily mean a wounded beast to follow up, especially if you were using a small-bore rifle. And, when following up a wounded buffalo in thick cover—and he will make for thick cover always when wounded—a powerful rifle is very necessary. For I doubt if there is another animal on the face of the earth quite so vindictive or quite so fiendishly determined as a wounded African buffalo can be.

As an example of this, the following incident is worth quoting. I cannot verify the facts, but from my own knowledge and experience of buffalo I see no reason whatever for doubting its veracity:

A hunter (very foolishly) went out one day entirely by himself and wounded in the body a large buffalo bull. The beast cleared off, and the man proceeded to follow it up. He caught sight of the bull as he came through a clump of grass and heading for a small waterhole. There were a few stunted trees about, and the grass between

him and the waterhole was short.   The bull was obviously
very hard hit, as he was travelling very slowly and painfully,
his body all hunched up.   He was making for the water.
But before he reached it, " A " gave him another shot in
the body, too far back to find either heart or lungs.   The
bull broke into a gallop, swung round in a small circle
and stopped.   " A ", closing in with the intention of
finishing off the wretched beast, suddenly found himself
being charged furiously from a range of about 40 or 50
paces.   He blazed off a couple of shots from his magazine
(he was using either a 9·3 mm. or a 10·75 mm. Mauser
of Continental origin and similar ammunition) but without
any apparent effect.   Then, as the bull was practically
on him, he dropped his rifle and scrambled up a convenient tree.   The bull pulled up, savaged the rifle a few
times, but without damaging it to any extent, and then
prowled round and round the tree, snorting, tossing his
head, pawing the ground and looking savagely up at
the hunter in the branches.

Presently he drew off a little way, and " A ", thinking
to slip quietly down the tree and get his rifle, commenced
to do so.   But at the first move the bull was back again,
and once more took up his patrol round and round the
tree.   At length, as the hunter kept perfectly motionless,
the bull again drew off ; and, as the sun was warming
up, he must have been suffering considerably from his
wounds, he apparently felt the call of the water irresistible.
He commenced to make slowly for the waterhole, stopping
every now and again to look round at the tree.   Now
the waterhole was only about 50 paces away ; but " A "
was too impatient to wait until the bull had actually
reached it.   He again attempted to clamber down and
get his rifle, and, although he was as quiet as possible,
the buffalo heard him, swung round and came galloping
back again.   This time he kept up his patrol round the
tree for close on half an hour ; then drew off 20 or 25
paces or thereabouts, and stood facing his enemy.

Now that buffalo must have been almost mad with thirst—" A " tells me that several times the animal's head turned round towards the water as though the temptation to drink was more than he could bear ; for the water was not more than 25 paces away from him—yet, right through the heat of the day, he stood there. It was the middle of the afternoon before the bull moved, and then it was only to lie down. Thinking that his strength had at last weakened, " A " again attempted to climb down. But, alas ! for his hopes, no sooner did he move than the bull was on his feet again ; though he did not otherwise move. Another hour went by ; and the bull again lay down.

" A ", giving up all hope of escaping, settled himself to wait and trusted that his boys would follow him up and, perhaps, succeed in driving off the bull. The sun went down, and, as the darkness closed in, " A " thought that he might manage to slip down the tree now. But no sooner did he attempt to do so, than his first movement was answered by an angry grunt from the buffalo. So he was compelled to abandon the attempt. An exceedingly uncomfortable night followed ; and, as at length the dawn appeared, " A " was able to make out the dark shape of the wounded bull precisely where he had been the previous evening. But, in the grey light of early dawn, he could not see any too clearly, so—after a day and a night without a bite to eat or a drop to drink, to say nothing of the stiffness which was his after a day and a night spent in the branches of a small tree—" A " just thought that he would remain where he was for the present.

Eventually, as the light increased, the hunter was able to make out the bull. He was still lying down facing the tree with his nose on the ground but with his body upright like a cow chewing the cud. " A " then broke branches, shouted and generally made as much noise as possible ; but there was no response from the bull. So he climbed

6

stiffly down from his perch, picked up his rifle and placed a bullet between the beast's eyes—just to make doubly sure. But the shot was not necessary ; the bull had died during the night.

Now this is just an example of the deadly determination which is such a characteristic of this species when wounded. That beast must have suffered agonies from thirst ; bearing in mind that he had received two bullets through the belly and that the smell of the water was in his nostrils all day telling him that there was, at least temporary, relief immediately behind him. Yet he put up with all that and died at his post rather than forgo his revenge. . . .

A wounded buffalo is the only beast which, when charging, I have never known to be turned. An elephant, a rhino, a lion—they can all be turned. A charging elephant, even if he is not knocked down, provided that a reasonably heavy bullet is used, will certainly be turned. And if you knock down or turn a charging elephant you seem to knock all the fight out of him for the time being —of course, if you follow him up and he knows that you are coming, he will probably ambush you again ; but that is an entirely different matter. After being stopped or turned his one idea seems to be to get away out of it.

A charging lion, if knocked down, may or may not attempt to press home the charge. It depends to a very great extent on how close he is to you : he may do so, but, on the other hand, he may attempt to slink away. But in my experience, and in that of every other hunter with whom I have ever discussed them, there is only one thing that will stop a charging buffalo : and that is, death —either his or yours.

All this to show how very necessary it is that you should carry a powerful rifle when hunting or following up a wounded buffalo. I do not think that a beginner should ever tackle buffalo at close quarters with a rifle showing less than 50 knock-out values. For it must be remem-

bered that the boss of a buffalo's horns—where they meet
in the centre of his forehead—is, for all practical purposes,
bullet-proof for anything save an extremely powerful rifle :
I have had a solid bullet (German) from a 10·75 mm.
(·423) Mauser blow to pieces on the boss of a big buffalo
bull's horns. I had wounded him in the body and when
following him up found him waiting for me in a place
where I was able to spot him in time ; I fired again, but
thanks to the fact that I was using that brute of an old
double-hammer weapon which I have already described,
I only succeeded in breaking a foreleg. The bull collapsed, and then started struggling to his feet again.
Disgusted with the old rifle, I exchanged it for the
10·75 mm. Mauser and opened fire with it ; but owing to
his struggles my first shot, intended to take him between
the eyes, struck him on the boss of the horns instead.
He took not the slightest notice, and had I not heard
the smack of the bullet, I should have thought that I
had clean missed him. As he reached his feet, I gave
him another between the eyes. On examining him, I
was astounded to find that my first bullet had dis-
integrated on impact with the horns : there was just a
leaden blotch to show where it had hit, exactly like the
leaden blotch you would find on a rough-surfaced rock
if you fired a plain lead bullet at it. It had not even
knocked him down, much less knocked him out. Accordingly, I do not consider that the 10·75 mm. (·423) is a
safe weapon to take against buffalo ; and the same remark
applies to the 11·2 mm. (·440).

A great many fatalities can be traced to the bullet-proof
qualities of this boss on a buffalo's horns. Men wound
a buffalo, follow him up, and then give him a shot in the
head as he charges. He drops, apparently stone dead ;
and the hunter sits down close by and lights cigarette
or a pipe, his rifle, in all probability, leaning up against
the buffalo's body. And the next thing is that the buffalo
—which was only stunned, through the bullet striking

the boss of his horns and failing to penetrate—has come-to and is trampling, pounding, and savaging the hunter to death.

If you have wounded the animal in the body, when he charges his head will be fairly steady ; but if your first shot smashed a shoulder, a leg, or a hip, he will be charging on three legs and consequently his head will be inclined to bob up and down as he comes, thereby offering a very much more difficult target. And remember, although he may be coming on three legs only, he will be coming at an altogether incredible speed.

It is absolutely imperative that the rifle should have sufficient power to knock him down even though the bullet may not be too well placed; no low-powered weapon can be relied upon to do so. A powerful double rifle is undoubtedly the best weapon for use in thick cover ; though a good magazine, provided that it throws a reasonably heavy bullet, can be used with perfect safety. Nevertheless, although it can be used with safety, it must not be imagined from that that it can therefore be used with an equal degree of satisfaction. I am very emphatic in declaring that it cannot. And the reason for this is to be found in the fact that a magazine rifle can only be so loaded that one type of bullet and one type of bullet only is ready for immediate use ; whereas, with a double, you can load a solid in one barrel and an expanding bullet in the other, either of which can be fired first at will. Of course, if you are following a wounded beast into thick cover you will load your rifle with solids irrespective of the type of weapon ; but when hunting a large herd it is not merely preferable but, I think, almost essential to load a solid in one barrel and an expanding bullet in the other. Because if you fire a solid bullet from a powerful rifle on a broadside shot at a buffalo standing with other members of the herd just beyond him, the bullet will almost certainly go clean through him and, almost equally certainly, wound at least one and possibly several of his companions. So that now you may find yourself with perhaps three or four wounded buffalo all round you in the thick bush or long grass, and you not knowing how hard they are hit nor whether they are likely to be close by or far away ; and when following one may find yourself being charged by another from a totally unexpected direction, you not having had the remotest idea that there was another within miles.

Another point to be borne in mind is the buffalo's propensity—it might almost, I think, be called a definite characteristic—for stampeding down-wind. If you have been closing the herd up-wind and open fire, both you and your trackers stand a very good chance of being run down—if it is a large herd—if you cannot succeed in splitting the herd so that it thunders past on both sides of you. No greater mistake can be made than to tackle any dangerous game at close quarters with a low-powered rifle or a cheap, mass-production weapon which may let you down at any moment. And, of course, the same remarks apply equally to your ammunition.

Although many buffalo are killed with medium-bore rifles—and there is no doubt that these weapons can be used with perfect satisfaction if the buffalo are in the open (which they very seldom are)—nevertheless, I consider that 400 grains is the minimum weight of bullet which ought ever to be taken against buffalo in thick cover ; and the heavier the bullet the better.

Generally speaking, throughout Africa the favourite rifles for buffalo in thick cover are doubles in the ·450– ·470-bore group ; whilst the double ·400 is widely used. Amongst the magazine enthusiasts, the ·404 and ·416 are probably the most popular.

Many men will tell you that solid bullets only should be used for buffalo, and for a number of years I agreed with them ; but subsequent experience convinced me that that advice is wrong, as I have endeavoured to show

when discussing the relative merits of double and magazine rifles for buffalo hunting. Pointed solid bullets
are not satisfactory owing to their tendency to glance
and turn over after entering, particularly should they
happen to encounter a bone ; the bluff-nosed solid is the
only kind that should ever be used.

With regard to expanding bullets : soft-nosed bullets
under 480 grains should have the lead barely showing
at the nose ; if there is too much lead exposed the bullet
may set up too soon if it encounters a large bone and so
fail to penetrate sufficiently. Bullets ranging upwards
from 480 grains should have plenty of lead showing. If
Westley Richards's capped bullets are used, the round
capped should be chosen ; because, on account of its
design, it does not set up so quickly as the pointed
" L.T." capped which is intended for rapid expansion,
and therefore has deeper penetration.

To sum up, then :

The best weapon for buffalo hunting in thick cover is
a double rifle throwing a bullet of not less than 400 grains ;
and the heavier the bullet the better. In the open a
medium-bore or large-medium-bore magazine rifle will
be found quite satisfactory.

If a magazine rifle is preferred at all times, it can be
used with a reasonable degree of safety, but not too much
satisfaction, provided it throws a bullet of not less than
400 grains.

CHAPTER VII

Rifles for Lion Hunting

THE principal remark which applies to rifles for elephant hunting, applies equally to rifles for all other dangerous game : the mere capacity to kill, *alone*, is insufficient.

A lion is not a particularly large beast ; whilst he definitely comes within the " soft-skinned " category. Any modern rifle will kill a lion, if the lion is obliging enough to give you a clear shot at his heart. But, as I have stated in a previous chapter, in good game country the solitary lion is definitely the exception. And, although you may succeed in killing one or more out of a pride with your light rifle, if you are attacked by any of the remainder you cannot rely on any light rifle to stop them. You may place your little bullets beautifully central ; they may pierce the heart through and through ; but—*they will not stop the lion.* And I do not think that it will be of much consolation to you to know that you have succeeded in killing a lion with a light rifle, if the lion has first succeeded in killing you ! Admittedly, a small bullet in the brain will kill instantaneously ; but the man has yet to be born who can be absolutely certain of placing his bullet in the brain of a charging lion.

A charging lion is a very different proposition from a charging elephant or buffalo. They, both of them, are, in the first place, very much larger targets, and come fairly steadily ; but a lion charges in a series of long, low bounds and so offers an extremely tricky target. In very open country in which the grass is short enough to enable you to kneel or squat down for the shot, a charging lion is not too difficult ; but in scrub country with longer grass he is just about as difficult as anybody could wish. So by all means if you like a light rifle, open fire with it if the lion are in the open ; but it is imperative that you should have a more powerful weapon beside you for use in the event of a charge, when the large-bore has a more immediate stopping effect than the small-bore.

My bag of oats will come in handy again here : If you stand a bag of oats up on a tree-stump and prod a packing needle into it, you will not knock that bag over ; but if you prod it hard with a walking stick you will knock it over, simply because of the vastly greater resistance which it encounters owing to its much larger diameter.

Since it may be desirable, if not necessary, to fire several shots in rapid succession if the lion are in the open, a magazine rifle has many obvious advantages, and is generally preferred for this work. But when following up a wounded lion, even if you know—that is, if you are as certain as you can be of anything in the African Bush— that you have placed your bullet centrally in his heart, a double-barrelled weapon is absolutely essential. The lion may be, and very probably is, dead ; but—you do not know for certain. He may still have a final kick left in him.

Colonel Patterson, in his fascinating account of the *Man-Eaters of Tsavo*, describes how he shot a lion which collapsed on its side and lay still. A number of Patterson's followers then rushed up and stood chatting in a group round the lion, which was apparently stone dead. But, just as Patterson himself arrived on the scene and was on the point of putting down his rifle so as to examine the lion, the beast scrambled to its feet and made a savage rush at one of Patterson's followers, chasing him up a tree. Colonel Patterson unfortunately omits to tell us where the first bullet had taken the lion ; but I gather that it must have struck a trifle high, and probably just grazed one of the projections on the under side of the spine. His

favourite rifle was a magazine ·303 ; though he admitted
that it lacked power—which is more than most men will
do where their pet rifles are concerned !

Blaney Percival, in his delightful and most informative
Game Ranger's Note Book, describes a somewhat similar
incident that happened to him. I have, myself, on several
occasions dropped various of the larger species of antelope
in just such a manner and have been astonished to find
that, after my boys had cut off the tail and were in the
act of cutting the beast's throat, that the animal has
suddenly come-to. Which serves to show how imperative it is that no matter what the animal, but particularly
where dangerous game are concerned, you should never
move your feet from the spot upon which you were
standing when you fired without first reloading your
rifle. And then always, always, advance towards the
animal with your rifle ready for instant use. If you
make a habit of this with all game, even if it is only a
guinea-fowl or a wild-goose, it will become instinctive
with you, and you will do so automatically when tackling
dangerous game : there will be no fear of you forgetting.

I have been reading the account of an incident which
took place in Northern Rhodesia. A sportsman was out
shooting lion somewhere beyond Livingstone. He had
shot a dozen or so altogether, and so might, not unreasonably, be expected to know something about the game ;
even if he did not, surely his common sense should have
told him how foolish he was. He had come across a
troop of lion and had shot four or five of them, using a
light magazine rifle (a ·275). One, he wounded. It
sprang into a clump of long grass. Now this sportsman
had a heavy rifle with him. I do not know what type
of weapon it was ; but " heavy rifle " in Africa usually
refers to a double in the ·450–·470-bore group. Now if
ever he was going to use that double, surely this was an
occasion that not merely called, but literally screamed,
for it ? But no ! he left the double with his gunbearer

and advanced into the long grass carrying his little light magazine rifle, and not even a knife on his belt ! But that is not all : *he had not even reloaded his rifle !* One gathers that there was a cartridge or two in the magazine, but he had not pushed one up the spout. It is difficult to believe ; but those are the facts as reported. The lion was crouching just within the grass : sprang on him : pulled him down : and commenced chewing his leg. His own words were : that the lion did not give him time to reload ! Presumably, therefore, he had entered the grass with an unloaded rifle in his hands ! Of course, this must be an exceptional case ; frankly, had I not seen the account of it, myself, in the paper, I could not have believed it.

Even supposing, for the sake of argument, that the account that I read was inaccurate and that the man had fired one shot at the lion, but had not *then* had time to reload ; the question still arises : Why was he not using his heavy double rifle ? Although there might not have been time in which to reload from the magazine, there would surely have been time in which to slip his finger from one trigger to the other on the double. Besides, the heavier bullet from the double would in all probability, in the first place, have knocked the lion down and so allowed ample time for a second shot. The hunter lost his leg, and might have easily lost his life ; but his gun-bearer—who had never fired a rifle in his life, but had an idea as to how they worked—rushed up to the lion, jammed the muzzles of the rifle against his head, and heaved on the triggers until the thing went off.

A very stout effort !

(Since writing the above, I have received the sportsman's own account of the incident : It appears that he did *not* enter the grass with an unloaded rifle ; but that, failing to stop the lion with one shot from the ·275, he turned to grab the double ·450 only to find that the boy carrying it had bolted. He then turned back to face the lion, and now had no time in which to reload. His old farm boy, seeing the local native bolting with the heavy rifle, snatched it from him and returned to rescue his master.)

The double-barrelled weapon is out and away the best type of weapon to use when following up a wounded lion. On this point there can be no two opinions—no two possible opinions. The infinitely better balance of a double permits of its being swung, mounted, and fired with greater rapidity, *combined with accuracy*, than could ever be possible with a magazine—assuming equally good weapons in either case.

When following up a wounded lion, the advantage is with him. He is motionless, whereas you are moving; he will certainly hear you as you come through the grass; but you, as yet, have no accurate idea as to his where-abouts. But, and this is just the point, the instant before he charges he will usually loose a savage snarl. From then until he launches himself forward in his charge, is only a matter of a split second. But that snarl gives you the direction in which to look. If you are carrying a double, you will very possibly be able to get in a shot during that split second; in other words, whilst the lion is still a stationary target. But, since an accurate shot from a magazine rifle cannot be fired with quite the same degree of rapidity, if you are carrying a weapon of this type, the lion may be actually under way before you have got your shot off. Consequently, he will be an extremely more difficult target; and, instead of being definitely knocked out, may be only momentarily dazed. It will depend entirely on how close he is to you, whether or not you will have time enough in which to reload from your magazine.

But with a double, even if the first shot is so badly placed that it fails to knock down the lion, but just as it were makes him pause, then because of the rapidity with which the second shot can be fired, you can slam the contents of the left barrel into him during that momentary pause. It will be noticed that I have been using the word " weapon ". I have done so on purpose, because it need not necessarily be a rifle. There are many men who have not the slightest intention of ever hunting elephant, and probably not even buffalo ; and therefore do not feel justified in ordering a double rifle just for use when follow-ing up an occasional, very occasional, wounded lion. But a 12-bore magnum " Paradox "-pattern ball-and-shot gun is a simply splendid weapon with which to back up your magazine rifle ; and, at the same time, is not, as it were, being wasted. Because besides being an extremely powerful rifle for close-range work against soft-skinned game, it is also a perfect shot gun. Although the ordinary 12-bore " Paradox " is a very serviceable weapon, it is nothing like so powerful as the magnum. In fact, to my mind, a 12-bore magnum " Paradox ", " Explora ", " Jungle Gun ", or whatever any particular gunsmith may call it, is an ideal weapon for the beginner to use when after lion (or for any man to use when after leopard), because if you have never previously faced a charging lion, it is rather an awe-inspiring experience. And this, coupled with your very natural excitement, to say nothing of the trace of equally natural and perfectly excusable nervousness which you may also be feeling—remember this is your first lion—is not going to tend to steady you. If the beast is very close, and you endeavour to take a snap-shot, you may fire before your sights are really and truly covering a vital spot. And this is where the great advantage of the magnum " Paradox " comes in. If you carry the right barrel loaded with large slugs (anything from L.G. to S.S.G.) a greater margin of error is per-missible than when a single bullet is used. If the slugs fail to kill, they will at least stop the beast, and then you can give him the big, heavy bullet from the left barrel whilst he is more or less motionless. The whole secret of stopping with absolute certainty a charging lion is to let him get close. Do not be in a hurry to fire. Provided that you have a powerful and thoroughly reliable weapon in your hands, there is not the slightest necessity for you to feel frightened. The closer the lion approaches, the bigger he seems and, therefore, the easier he is to hit. Do not fire your first shot until he is within 10 or 12 paces ; give him the slugs then, and, if they fail to kill, you can hardly miss him at that range with the bullet from the left barrel.

(For the benefit of those who do not know the " Paradox " I might just mention that the principle of the gun is in having a short portion of the muzzle of the barrel rifled ; the remainder of the bore being smooth like an ordinary shot-gun. A weapon of this description only weighs about 8 lb. or thereabouts, and cannot therefore, by any possible stretch of the imagination, be termed heavy.)

In very open country, such, for instance, as the great open plains in parts of Kenya and Tanganyika—particularly Tanganyika, where the famous Serengetti Plains might almost be termed a breeding-ground for all the lions in Africa !—a powerful magazine rifle can be used with perfect satisfaction and more than a reasonable degree of safety. But, even on those open plains, there are clumps of grass here and there, and occasional small thickets of bush, into which a wounded lion can make his way, and therefore when a double rifle would be preferable with which to follow him up.

Few men in Africa, nowadays, carry a revolver. (I am not now considering the sport practised in Kenya of hunting lions on horseback, since, owing to horsesickness, tsetse-fly, and the nature of the country elsewhere, it is impracticable in other parts of the continent ; though its devotees in Kenya have evolved an etiquette and set of rules of their own which experience has shown to be best suited to their favourite sport, one of which is the carrying by each man of either a heavy revolver or automatic pistol.)   When hunting on foot, a revolver is a weapon which you may never need in a lifetime in the bush ; but, if you do need it, you are liable to need it badly. A revolver once saved my life when, for no reason at all, a leopard sprang on me from a tree : I was following a small game trail running down to the river—up Barotse-land way—about sun-down.   I was not hunting ; but just looking for a place near the river for the night's camp. There was a bough of a tree overhanging the path, and a thick bush in between which prevented me from seeing it.   The leopard was probably waiting for some beast to come along for a drink.   The wind was blowing across, so that he could not have known what was coming.   Then as I turned the corner round the bush, he may have so tensed himself for a quick spring that he overbalanced ; or possibly considered that he had, as it were, been trapped or cornered, and that attack was his only hope. I do not know ; all I do know is that some instinct made me look up, and I found myself gazing into the wide-open mouth and blazing eyes of a leopard whose face was not more than about a foot from mine, as he launched himself down on top of me.   There was no avoiding him.   He landed on my chest, and I went down under him.   How-ever, I had had time in which to yank out the old ·455 Webley which I always carried in those days.   I did not, though, have time in which to shove it into his mouth as I should have liked to have done ; but was compelled to fire into his chest with the muzzle of the revolver touching him.   The bullet took him through the heart ; but, as usual, it was some little while before he died— and during that short while he was not idle !   I could not help myself, because as I went down my helmet flew off and the back of my head made contact with a stone, which scattered my wits.   My last recollection was of moving my head slightly to one side in an endeavour to save my ear from being chewed off.   For the leopard was lying on my chest, his head and mine being cheek by jowl ;

and I had no difficulty in hearing his jaws clashing just beside that ear of mine.

The youngster who was carrying my rifle ran up when he heard the shot, saw me lying under the leopard, and, without an instant's hesitation, brought the butt of the rifle down, hard, on the brute's head. It was an extremely plucky thing to do, for the lad had no means of knowing that the brute was at his last gasp. It smashed the butt off the rifle, but it also finally put a stop to the leopard's antics ; which was, perhaps, just as well, because the ribs down the right side of my chest were all exposed (I was mighty lucky not to be dis-embowled), whilst the flesh of my right thigh was in ribbons : though by some miracle the femoral artery was untouched.

On another occasion, in the Lower Zambezi Valley, I had shot and killed four lions out of a troop of five, and wounded the fifth—a lioness. She sprang into a clump of long grass, and I proceeded to follow her up. My rifle was a short, sporting, Martini-Henry which is, of course, a single-shot weapon. I came on the lioness, and the instant that she saw me she charged from a range of about 12 or 15 paces. I fired ; knocked her down ; but failed to kill her. She scrambled to her feet and was on me before I had completed reloading. As she reared up to grab me, I drove the muzzle of the rifle as hard as I could into her mouth as though there had been a bayonet on the end of it. She dropped to the ground, choked, then grabbed the barrel in her teeth and whisked the rifle out of my hands as though it had been a straw, shook it, and tossed it to one side. But I had had time, by now, to draw my old Webley, and, when she came for me again, I was able to blow her brains out from a range of about one inch just as her jaws closed on my knee. She did not even draw blood ; though that was probably thanks to the fact that the long tushes at the corner of her mouth had been broken off flush with the gums.

Now I was mighty glad to have a revolver on both of those occasions ; although there have only been those two in twenty-five years of hunting, during which time I have hunted twelve months a year every year with but two short breaks of a few months each.   I must admit, however, that I do not carry a revolver nowadays ; though that is principally due to the fact that I spend considerably more time after elephant and buffalo now than ever I did before ; but it is also because I am using vastly better rifles now than I was in those far-off days. I really do not think that with modern high-power rifles it is necessary to carry a revolver nowadays.

To sum up, then :

The best weapon for lion hunting is a powerful double rifle—and the heavier the bullet the better when following up a wounded beast.

A magazine rifle can be used quite satisfactorily if the lion are in the open ; but if it is a light weapon, then a more powerful weapon must be kept at hand in case of a charge.   A 12-bore magnum " Paradox "-pattern ball-and-shot gun is eminently suitable for this purpose; though a powerful rifle is, of course, better.

CHAPTER VIII

Hollands ·375 Magnum

I AM giving this rifle a chapter to itself because I honestly think that it deserves it, it is so far ahead of any of its contemporaries ; and because a discussion of its merits brings up a few points of intense interest, even though they are not really understood yet by anybody. All that any of us can do is to put forward our views and possible explanations in the light of our own experiences and hope that by doing so the real truth of the amazing, indeed phenomenal, killing power of this rifle may be sifted and the real reason for it made clear.

The killing power of the ·375 magnum is something that can only be properly appreciated by one who has actually used it himself on a large variety of game. Excluding head shots which miss the brain and therefore only stun the animal, I have never known an animal brought down by this rifle get to its feet again. It seems to have a paralysing effect. And that this effect is directly due to a high striking velocity cannot be seriously disputed. A comparison has only to be attempted between it and its predecessors, the old ·375's, when it will be immediately apparent that no comparison is possible. Yet the weight and diameter of the bullets is the same (assuming that the 270-grain bullet for the magnum is being chosen).

An intensely interesting discussion, in which I took a small part, ran through the pages of that splendid, fine journal, *Game and Gun*, during 1936 and 1937 and into 1938 on this question of " Bullet Velocity and Killing Power ", and in which the ·375 magnum was unanimously admitted to be the outstanding example. Various suggestions were put forward by correspondents and contributors to account for this paralysing effect which proves so deadly—literally instantaneous death following on the shot for all the world as though the animal had been shot through the brain or had had its neck broken.

It was shown that smaller calibres also possess this peculiar property of paralysing an animal, provided their striking velocities were sufficiently high and, most important, that their little light bullets were only used on the little light animals for which they were designed and intended. Because, if used on heavier animals, they tended to blow to pieces on impact and thus dissipated their power before reaching the vital zones.

And this is where the utility of the ·375 magnum begins to become apparent. Because its three different weights of bullet have been specially designed to cover practically every species of animal on the face of the earth. And, from the lightest to the heaviest, they all three have a splendidly high striking velocity. Further, thanks to their well-chosen weight and shape, there is no fear of any one of them disintegrating on any animal in the groups for which they are intended (or even, indeed, much heavier animals). And it is this that makes the ·375 magnum such an outstandingly useful weapon : the exceptionally wide range of animals that can be killed cleanly, easily and with despatch, by the one weapon. In addition to all of which, it has a flatter trajectory and a higher striking velocity at any range than any of its contemporaries firing bullets of even approximately similar weight, shape and diameter. And on top of all that, there is the additional fact that all these three bullets can be fired from the same weapon without any alteration in the sighting or aim being necessary.

There is no other weapon in existence of which so much can be said ; and when it is further remembered that the rifle can be obtained as double, single and magazine, so that all tastes are catered for and all types of shooting considered ; it must surely be admitted that here is, indeed, a weapon which every man—or woman —wanting a rifle must at least consider.

After reading this eulogy, it may be wondered why I only tentatively mentioned the suitability of the ·375 magnum for use against the various animals discussed in the previous chapters. I did that most particularly because there are many men who, having been disappointed in the past with the behaviour of the old ·375's, are now biased against anything of that calibre and will not allow themselves to believe that the ·375 magnum can possibly be all that its supporters claim for it. For instance, to mention but one complaint sometimes heard, I have known more than one man complain that the ·375 (9·5 mm.) Mannlicher-Schonauer lacked penetration, as a result of which many wounded animals were lost; and they feared that they might experience the same thing with the ·375 magnum.

Quite apart from soft-skinned game, I have killed quite a few buffalo—massive-boned animals weighing upwards of a ton—with the 270-grain semi-pointed soft-nosed bullet from the ·375 magnum, only firing the one shot at each. Further, I have instantly killed a large bull hippo with the same bullet, hitting him behind the ear, on an occasion when I had no solids with me. As far as the 300-grain solid bullet is concerned, I have, on not a few occasions, manœuvred into a suitable position so as to get two buffalo in line and dropped them both with but a single shot: and these were not body shots; I put the bullet through the nearest bull's head and then into his companion's neck, when the bullet still had sufficient power left to smash it. I have several times had three buffalo dead to one bullet—heart shot. But the biggest bag of all was seven eland to one shot! (An eland may weigh from 15 cwt. upwards). I did not intend to do it; in fact, I did not know that there were any others besides the one bull that I saw at the edge of the bush on the opposite side of a small clearing. I happened to be loaded with solids, so let rip, shooting him through the heart ; and when I got there found five more lying dead in the bush beyond and one with its back broken ; after which the bullet had passed through a tree about 5 inches in diameter and then gone on.   But the most outstanding example of penetration that I have ever seen took place within a hundred yards of where I am typing this : A native from over the border had been visiting me here in my camp.   He left about midday to return to his home ; but only ten minutes or so after bidding me farewell, he came running back to tell me that there were two immense buffalo bulls close by.   I grabbed the nearest rifle, which happened to be a ·375 magnum, and went out with him.   Not a hundred yards away, the lad stopped and whispered that it was here that he had seen the two bulls.   There were some stunted trees scattered about, and the grass was only about 3½ feet high ; one would have thought that there was hardly sufficient cover to conceal small buck never mind two great buffalo.   However, I had confidence in the boy, so walked slowly towards the spot indicated with my rifle ready for instant use.   When some 15 or 20 paces away, I halted and whistled quietly, as though wishing to attract somebody's attention without rousing the whole countryside.   Nothing happened ; so I whistled again a trifle more loudly and insistently.   And then I saw it. Ever so slowly and carefully, so as not to expose himself more than was absolutely necessary, one of the bulls raised his head to look and see if there was really anything to worry about, or whether it might not just be one native calling to another over nothing at all.   All I could see was the points of the beautifully curved horns, the massive boss in the centre, and a black patch in the grass below the boss.   I raised my rifle and fired into the grass centrally below the boss and just where I knew his fore-head must be.   The horns disappeared ; and a mighty beast sprang up out of the grass some 5 or 6 yards farther away. I knew that this must be the second bull, and dropped him with a shot through the shoulders. I then advanced towards the first one with my rifle ready for instant action, as I did not know whether he was dead or only knocked out. However, I found that my bullet had taken him fairly between the eyes and that he was as dead as a kippered herring. As my boy cut off his tail, however, he called to me to come and look. He wanted to show me the bullet hole beside the root of the bull's tail where my bullet had made its exit. Now I have many times seen rifles of different calibres drive solid bullets clean through buffalo on frontal chest shots ; but I had never previously seen any rifle drive a bullet from between a big buffalo bull's eyes, through his head, down his neck, right through his body, and then make its exit alongside the root of his tail.

In case anybody feels like raising a sceptical eyebrow over this, I might just mention that at the time I had a certain very exalted personage in camp who had retained my professional services as hunter, interpreter and guide, etc., for a hunting trip in this part of the world. Since he, and at least one member of his staff, was extremely keen on everything appertaining to rifles, it goes without saying that we had many discussions on the relative merits of our favourite weapons ; and so it came about that both these persons came to examine the buffalo, not only because it was such an interesting example of how successfully such huge beasts could hide themselves, but also to see for themselves the really extraordinary penetration of the ·375 magnum. I am not mentioning these sportsmen's names here as they might not like it ; but shall be pleased to do so to any bona-fide enquirer.

Which should, I think, remove any doubts concerning the penetrative powers of the ·375 magnum. But it was because of those doubts that I feared that if I was too free with suggestions for its use in the commencement, these men might condemn everything I have to say to the beginner as the vapourings of a small-bore enthusiast (which I, most emphatically, am not). Particularly in view of the fact that I am regretfully compelled to admit that even my own " Knock-Out " values do not do adequate justice to the power of this rifle.

And this brings me back to that discussion to which I have already referred, which ran through *Game and Gun.* It was there suggested in one exceptionally well-thought-out, closely-reasoned and carefully-worded article that the peculiar property of shock possessed by the ·375 magnum was the outcome of weight and diameter of bullet in conjunction with speed and depth of penetration ; the combination of these factors producing a phenomenon of " shock " differing in its features from any with which we are usually acquainted. The sportsman, who modestly conceals his identity under the cypher " 577 ", wrote as follows :

> . . . That the passage of a projectile of that [minimum] diameter, at that high velocity, through tissues of high liquid content, sets up a violent " wave " [of pressure or oscillation] at right angles to its course and against the inertia of the surrounding tissues. This " wave " of mechanical shock, transmitted through and indefinitely far around the tissues about the axis of the bullet's course, directly [and more extensively than the bullet itself could] affects the functions of all vital structures and elements it reaches—in short, a blow against all the minute cells comprising living tissues—but, without causing as much visible local laceration as certain expanding, or disrupting, bullets of smaller bore and higher velocity are known to.

That was the theory put forward for examination ; and I am convinced that it contains the secret of the amazing power of the ·375 magnum ; and, perhaps, why no figures or formulas can accurately indicate its capabilities. And it was because my " K-O " values do not do full justice to the power of this rifle that I was very chary of recommending it before I had had an opportunity of thoroughly discussing it ; particularly in view of the fact that according to the tables the 10·75 mm. (·423) would appear to be a more suitable weapon, whereas practical experience has convinced me that it cannot be compared with the ·375 magnum from any point of view (but I shall discuss this more fully in the next chapter).

I know, from using the rifle myself, that the ·375 magnum can safely and satisfactorily be taken against any animal anywhere in Africa. This is not written on the strength of shooting a few beasts with a new weapon and being pleased with the result. I have had three of Holland's ·375 magnums : the first bought secondhand in the early days of my experiments ; after using it extensively I discarded it in order to try other weapons ; later, after I had been through the list of its contemporaries, I bought another, also secondhand, so as to check up on the notes that I had made on the first one's behaviour. So satisfied was I that I then discarded it and had Messrs. Holland & Holland build me up a new one—the one that I am using at present. I have fired more ·375 magnum ammunition in my life than any other calibre : over 5,000 rounds at game, including all kinds of African game from elephant downwards.

I kept no record of the number of elephant and buffalo shot with the first two ·375 magnums ; but I distinctly remember the day when this one dropped its hundredth elephant ; and in addition this same one has accounted for somewhere between 400 and 500 buffalo, besides a number of rhino, hippo and lion, and, of course, a fair quantity of lesser game. So that both it and I are thoroughly accustomed to each other's little ways. I am not suggesting for a moment that it alone is a suitable weapon for the professional elephant hunter ; and naturally I have other much more powerful weapons for use under certain conditions. But what I am suggesting is that personal experience has shown me that it is an eminently safe, sound and intensely-satisfactory weapon to take against any animal anywhere if the sportsman does not want to be bothered with a number of different weapons.

CHAPTER IX

An " All-round " Rifle

A VAST number of men, not merely beginners, are constantly seeking the ideal " all-round " rifle. That is, a weapon which can be satisfactorily used for all purposes and against all kinds of game. But, like most other ideals, it is mighty difficult of attainment.

If the foregoing chapters have been studied, it will be immediately obvious that no rifle can really be considered a genuine " all-round " weapon unless it is double-barrelled ; because, as I trust I have already made sufficiently clear, there are purposes for which the double is so infinitely preferable to any magazine that its use is practically essential under certain conditions and for certain types of hunting. And I know that if I had to finish the remainder of my career with but one rifle and one rifle only, it would have to be double-barrelled ; I would not consider any magazine on the market, save under protest and the utmost necessity ; nor, were I compelled to continue hunting with a magazine, could I possibly do so with anything like the same confidence.

However, I am fully aware that in Africa, at any rate, I am very much of a lone voice crying in the wilderness —a wilderness of cheap, mass-production magazines— when trying to recommend a double for all purposes to the man who only wants to use one rifle ; and so I shall set forth the pros and cons of all those rifles which are generally used by the " one-rifle " man and which are frequently described as " all-round " rifles, so that the advantages claimed for one can be compared with those claimed for another. But before coming to the rifles themselves, there are a few points in connection with the conditions under which they will be used which call for

remark so that there will be no fear of their being overlooked or forgotten, when it comes to deciding on the rifle.

The delightful uncertainty as to what species of game
you are next going to meet is generally considered as being
one of the greatest fascinations of African hunting : every
next step you take in bush or scrub country may bring
you face to face with some great wild creature : it may
be an elephant or an eland ; a reed-buck or a rhino ; a
buffalo or a warthog ; anything at all, from the biggest
to the smallest ; you cannot tell.   Accordingly, I cannot
for the life of me see how a man can possibly hope to hunt
satisfactorily under such conditions with a magazine rifle.
Because the point that the advocates of this type of
weapon do not seem to realize is, that a magazine rifle
can only be loaded so that one type of bullet, and one
only, is ready for instant use.   Consequently, if you are
carrying your rifle loaded with ammunition suitable for
soft-skinned game, with the usual contrariness of things,
it will almost certainly be thick-skinned animals which
you will encounter first, and vice versa.   And since you
may, and probably will, encounter them at fairly close
quarters and without the slightest warning, if you set-to
to change the cartridges in your rifle you will almost
certainly stampede them.   I am fully aware that all good
magazine rifles nowadays have a spring clip in the front
of the trigger-guard for, in the words of the gunsmiths' catalogues, the purpose of instantly emptying the
magazine when it is desired to change the cartridges for
a different type of bullet.   Well, I have yet to be present
when this operation is performed without the most appalling clatter ; no self-respecting wild animal within half
a mile would stay to see the end of the performance.   It
is on this account that I maintain that if you must use
magazine rifles, then two of them are necessary : one
loaded with expanding bullets, and the other with bluff-
nosed solids ; you carry yourself the one that you think
you are most likely to require, and your gunbearer carries

the other. But this, of course, is getting away from the idea of an " all-round " rifle.

In contrast to the foregoing, a double can be carried with two different types of bullet ready for immediate use. And not only that, but if it is desired to draw one of those cartridges and substitute another when close to game, you can do so in absolute silence : it will not be necessary for you to creep away to a safe and suitable distance where the animals will not hear you, and then stalk up again, thus giving the beasts a double, in fact, treble, opportunity of spotting you.

However, taking it on the whole, there is less difficulty in finding a rifle suitable for all types of general African hunting than is the case in India, where the two main types of shooting are so widely different and where the very conditions under which the animals themselves are usually shot are also so different. Generally speaking, African hunting comes, as it were, midway between the two main Indian extremes of Hill-shooting and Jungle-shooting.

One of the principal arguments usually put forward in favour of the magazine rifle is that in good game country lion are usually met in troops or prides, and that it is therefore necessary for the sportsman to be able to fire several shots in rapid succession. But I cannot see the force of this argument : I cannot see why the sportsman should *want* to fire a number of shots at them ; unless, of course, he is out for quantity instead of quality in respect of his bag ; which surely is the very antitheses of all that is usually implied in the term " sportsmanship ". If a man is shooting antelope, he picks his beast, drops him, and lets the rest go ; he does not rip off the contents of his magazine at the remainder of the troop. Then why is it that when he gets a troop of lion in front of him, he must endeavour to blot out everything he can see with hair on it irrespective of sex or anything else ? Yet I am afraid that this is what happens all too often ; and in his frantic haste to make a large bag before they clear off, he almost invariably succeeds in only wounding one or two over and above those he has killed   He will now have to follow up, and, as I have pointed out in the chapter dealing with lion, a double should always be used for this work.

Now at one time or another, practically every rifle on the market, from ·256 to ·440 (11·2 mm.), both inclusive, has been called an " all-round " rifle.   But, as I have endeavoured to show in the preceding chapters—and as I trust I have succeeded in doing—no small-bore, or rifle throwing a light bullet, can be safely used against dangerous game at close quarters.   And, since a genuine " all-round " rifle must be a suitable weapon for use both at close quarters as well as in the open, our choice is at once restricted to rifles delivering a knock-out blow of not less than 40 values—in other words of not less power than Holland's ·375 magnum.

(By the way, it will be noted that throughout this book when referring to the ·375 magnum I have almost invariably mentioned Holland's name at the same time. I have done so on purpose because Messrs. Holland & Holland designed and introduced this rifle and cartridge and although many other firms build ·375 magnums now, as far as I can gather from a study of their catalogues, there is a slight difference in the cartridges used in their rifles from those used in Holland's rifles.   And, whilst the ballistics of the 270-grain bullets are approximately the same, there appears to be an appreciable difference in the ballistics of the cartridges when loaded with the 300-grain bullet.   Accordingly, since I consider that Holland's ·375 magnum is the lowest-powered rifle that can be safely taken against dangerous game at close quarters, I have made a point of mentioning their name throughout so as to avoid any possibility of a misunderstanding and consequent disappointment.   If I am in error concerning this question of ·375 magnums built by other firms and the cartridges which their rifles fire, then the fault must lie with them and the ballistics which they quote in their catalogues.)

Now I am fully aware that a very great deal of dangerous game is killed every year in Africa with medium-powered rifles such as the ·318, ·333, ·350 magnum, ·366 (9·3 mm.), etc., all of which are widely used and are deservedly popular ; but that does not alter my contention that if you will use light bullets on dangerous game at close quarters, you may get away with it for years (as Bell did) ; but that you are asking for trouble, and that if you will persist in doing so you will most surely find it sooner or later, unless you are extremely lucky (as he was).   But it is worth bearing in mind that it is the exception which proves the rule.   Trouble is the one thing that you can be quite confident of receiving in this life if you persist in asking for it.   You can make mistakes indefinitely when shooting rabbits and suffer no particular inconvenience ; but what so many men seem to forget is, that you cannot defy and continue to defy a brooding Nemesis where dangerous game are concerned without sooner or later being called to account.

Besides, there is another point which, I deeply regret to have to say, is all too frequently forgotten—in fact, it never seems to enter the average sportsman's head at all in Africa—and that is, that you are almost invariably accompanied by a number, large or small, of unarmed natives : your trackers, gunbearers, lads carrying water and so on.   Now, you are perfectly at liberty to place yourself in as many tight corners as you like—and tackling dangerous game at very close quarters with very light bullets is little better than attempting suicide—you are even, and equally, at liberty to get yourself killed if you wish—it is entirely a matter for yourself, and in all probability nobody will care—but the point is that it is most unfair and most unsportsmanlike to expose those lads who accompany you to any sort of unnecessary risk whatsoever. You are just as responsible for them and their lives—though the fact does not appear to be sufficiently appreciated—as any subaltern is for the lives of the men in his platoon.

The only rifles, then, which can be considered as " all-round " rifles are :

·375 magnum (Holland)

This rifle can be had in either magazine or double-barrelled form. Since I have devoted the entire preceding chapter to a discussion of this rifle, it is not necessary for me to say much about it here beyond the fact that the light 235-grain bullet is excellent for the lighter varieties of soft-skinned game such as are generally shot at fairly long range ; the 270-grain bullet cannot be beaten for all the heavier varieties of soft-skinned game (with which lion in the open may be included) such as are generally shot at medium ranges ; and the 300-grain bullet, with its high striking velocity, deals a tremendous blow at close quarters and may safely be used against dangerous game. This rifle, then, has definitely been designed as an " all-round " rifle for the man who only wishes to use the one weapon on all kinds of game. The additional fact that all three weights of bullet can be fired from the one weapon without any alteration whatsoever being necessary in aim or sighting is an astounding thing in the case of a single-barrelled rifle, but is a thousand times more so in the case of a double, and reflects the greatest possible credit on the designers.

·369 (Purdey)

This rifle is only obtainable in double-barrelled form. For all practical purposes it is identical with Holland's ·375 magnum when the latter is firing the 270-grain bullet. But it only fires the one bullet and this being pointed would not be suitable in solid form. Obviously, therefore, it can only be considered as an " all-round " rifle where soft-skinned game are concerned.

·450/·400 (Jeffery and Purdey)

This is a double-barrelled rifle. For years, prior to the introduction of the ·375 magnum, this rifle had the reputation of being the weapon which most nearly met all requirements for general, all-round, big game hunting. It is still immensely and deservedly popular, particularly in its new 9½-lb. guise. I have used it extensively and used to swear by it—I still do. Throughout the length and breadth of Africa, I cannot remember ever hearing a man say a word against it. It is undoubtedly one of the most popular cartridges that has ever been placed on the market for general all-round big game hunting. The solid bullet is excellent for elephant and rhino ; with a solid in one barrel and a soft-nosed with lead just showing at the tip in the other, it is splendidly effective on buffalo ; while with soft-nosed bullets having plenty of lead showing at the nose, it is very deadly on lion ; for non-dangerous game, soft-nosed and soft-nosed-split bullets are used with great satisfaction on all but the smallest varieties. In fact, about the only genuine criticism that can be honestly levelled against the ·400-bore from the point of view of an " all-round " rifle is that the bullet is a trifle on the heavy side for the lighter varieties of soft-skinned game ; and that, perhaps, when compared with the ·375 magnum, its trajectory is not quite so flat as might sometimes be required in those parts of the world where comparatively small animals are occasionally shot at long ranges. However, I am principally concerned with Africa and African hunting, and there cannot be the slightest doubt that the ·400 has as flat a trajectory as could ever be needed for all normal African requirements where, in spite of all that you may hear to the contrary, it is very, very seldom that a shot has ever to be fired at more than 200 yards range, and where the animals usually shot are quite capable of stopping a 400-grain soft-nosed-split bullet.

I can also say, and say it with emphasis, that the ·400

is an eminently safe, sound, and splendidly satisfactory weapon to take against all dangerous African game any- where. I would not hesitate, with a Jeffery double ·400 in my hands, to tackle the heaviest or most dangerous animal in all Africa, in the densest of cover ; and, what is more, I should do so with every confidence.

When compared with the ·375 magnum from the point of view of all-round utility, the question really resolves itself into a consideration of the type of hunting in which the sportsman concerned principally expects to indulge. For the man who intends, or expects, to be usually shoot- ing the game found in fairly open country, but would like an occasional smack at the big fellows in the thick stuff, then the ·375 magnum is the obvious weapon to choose ; because for the greater part of this man's shoot- ing the variety of bullets and their more suitable weights for such work, in addition to the flatter trajectory and higher striking velocity of this rifle, would certainly prove more generally satisfactory. But if you think that you will be spending the greater part of your time after heavy and dangerous game in thick and fairly thick cover, but also doing a reasonable amount of work amongst non- dangerous game in less close country—which everybody in Africa has to do from time to time—then I honestly think that the ·400 will prove a better and more suitable weapon ; because there is no getting away from the fact that the heavier bullet thrown by the ·400 *does* hit a heavier blow at close quarters than does the bullet from the ·375 magnum, in spite of the latter's much higher striking velocity.

·404 (Jeffery)

This is a magazine rifle ; in fact Jeffery introduced it as the magazine edition of his so popular ·400-bore—the ballistics and trajectory are identical—and to take the place of the single-loader which was so widely used by those men who did not feel that they could afford a double.

I think one can safely say that it is the most widely-used calibre throughout the entire big game hunting world : you can hardly pick up a gunsmith's catalogue from any country, not merely Great Britain, without finding the ·404 listed. As far as its effectiveness is concerned, exactly the same remarks apply to it as to the ·400 ; the only difference being that it is a magazine and therefore not so suitable for certain types of hunting.

Recently, however, Jeffery introduced a new cartridge for it which brings it within the magnum group. An increased powder charge and a lighter bullet (300 grains) gives it a muzzle velocity of 2,600 f./s. with a corresponding muzzle energy of 4,500 ft.-lb. This makes it wonderfully effective on soft-skinned game and gives it as flat a trajectory as you are ever likely to require anywhere. At the same time, with all due respect to the designer, I cannot help thinking that he missed a wonderful opportunity by not providing a variety of bullets. The only bullets obtainable are pointed : solid pointed, which are useless for any kind of game shooting ; and copper pointed expanding, which tend to blow to pieces all too readily if they happen to encounter a heavy bone at close ranges. Jeffery tells me that he only intended this cartridge for use at the longer ranges, and that for dangerous game at close quarters the standard 400-grain bullet should be used. That, of course, is sound advice ; but a very considerable quantity of non-dangerous game is shot at close and fairly close ranges in Africa, on which semi-pointed soft-nosed and bluff-nosed soft-nosed bullets would be very deadly in view of the high striking velocity.

If the rifle is sighted, as it can be sighted, so that the 400-grain bullet shoots accurately at all ranges up to, say, 150 yards, and the 300-grain bullet used for soft-skinned game at ranges between 150 and 300 yards, this new cartridge greatly increases the scope of the ·404 for use in all parts of the world as an " all-round " rifle for those who for any reason prefer a magazine to a double.

Firing the 400-grain bullet, the ·404 has proved itself over and over again as being an eminently safe, sound and satisfactory weapon for all dangerous game from elephant downwards. The fact that all the highly efficient and exhaustively trained native hunters employed by the Governments of Uganda and Tanganyika for Elephant Control and Cultivation Protection are armed with ·404's, speaks, I think, for itself. Since, when the very considerable revenue derived from the sale of ivory shot in Cultivation Protection is borne in mind, there cannot be the slightest doubt that the Governments concerned could well afford to issue their men with more powerful rifles were such found to be necessary.

·405 (Winchester)

Magazine only. In spite of its calibre this rifle cannot be considered as a possible. It lacks power for dangerous game, and its trajectory is not sufficiently flat for all purposes. It is an out-of-date cartridge and action.

·416 (Rigby)

Rigby builds his ·416 in magazine form only. For all-round work amongst dangerous game, both thick-skinned and thin-skinned, there is no better magazine rifle than Rigby's ·416. I have never handled a magazine rifle of any sort, large-bore, medium-bore or small-bore, in which the feed from magazine platform to chamber was quite so delightfully smooth or required quite so little effort as on my Rigby ·416.

Those splendid steel-covered solid bullets which Rigby supplies for use with it, with their amazing thickness of solid steel at the nose, ensure that, no matter how massive the bone which it encounters, there can be no fear of the bullet loosing its shape and thereby its direction. With expanding bullets, its stopping power where lion are concerned is extraordinary.

Owing to its higher velocity, its trajectory curve is

8

somewhat flatter than that of the ·404 when the latter is
firing the standard 400-grain bullet, whilst it is definitely
a more powerful weapon.   With solid bullets on heavy
animals such as elephant, rhino and buffalo this additional
power is quite apparent but is not so obvious as when
soft-nosed bullets are being used on, say, lion, particularly
when it is a case of stopping a charge : the ·404 will stop
him all right, but will seldom crumple him quite so
completely as will the ·416.   Its ammunition, however,
is appreciably more expensive, and although personally
I consider that a very minor detail in an otherwise suitable
weapon, I am fully aware that the vast majority of men
will say that it is too expensive and the rifle too heavy and
costly for use against non-dangerous game, particularly in
the case of the man who only wants to use the one weapon.

·423 (10·75 mm.) Mauser

This is, of course, a magazine rifle.   It is one of life's
little mysteries to me how this rifle ever gained the popu-
larity which it undoubtedly possesses.   I suppose it is
because German rifles can be bought so cheaply in Africa
and elsewhere, because the ammunition is comparatively
cheap, and because it can be used with a certain amount
of safety and a modicum of satisfaction against most game.
Personally, however, I have no use for it whatsoever.
Even its staunchest supporters admit that it is incapable
of driving a bullet into an African elephant's brain from
in front ; it is not even able to drive a solid bullet through
a buffalo's shoulder : it will smash the shoulder, but will
not go through the bone to penetrate sufficiently far to
kill ; the buffalo, having been brought down for a few
moments, will then get to his feet and clear off with a
broken shoulder unless finished off at once.

I, myself, had a solid bullet (German) disintegrate on
the boss of a big buffalo bull's horns.   I had wounded
him too far back in the body to be immediately fatal, and
when following him up found him in a place where I

was able to see him before he saw me. It was a very
awkward shot, however, and I only managed to smash
his shoulder. This brought him down ; but before I
had torn my way through a matted tangle of bush and
closed in to make sure of him, he had got to his feet.
He charged, or rather tried to ; I let drive at his face,
but his head bobbed badly just as I squeezed the trigger
and had I not heard the smack of the bullet I should have
thought that I had missed him clean, because he took not
the slightest notice of the shot. I eventually killed him,
and examined him to see what had happened to that first
shot fired at his face. I found that it had taken him on
the boss of the horns and apparently blown to pieces :
there was just a leaden blotch for all the world as though
I had fired a revolver bullet at him !

One of the keenest upholders of this rifle recently
stated in a book he wrote that he generally used solid
bullets on eland and lion so as to ensure sufficient penetration to kill ; and he is a man with considerable experience.
Another says the same thing : that the 10·75 mm. soft-
nosed bullet is unable to drive through an eland's
shoulder. Well, I should never recommend a rifle for
a beginner or anybody else in which solids had to be
used for lion.

In fairness to this rifle, however, I must admit that
one assistant Game Warden in Kenya has shot over 300
elephant with a 10·75 mm. Mauser ; and a number of
men swear by it—others, like myself, swear at it. Still,
provided you get the rifle which is to fire it built for you
in England, the 10·75 mm. cartridge can, I suppose, be
considered as coming within the " all-round " category.
I presume that it must be possible to get a decent rifle
in Germany ; but I must admit that all those that I have
ever seen have been of the cheap, mass-production
variety, though some of them were of apparently better
quality than others. Nevertheless, it was one of those
seemingly better-class weapons that let me down that

time amongst the elephant as described in a previous chapter.

I admit that my admission of the 10·75 mm. into the ranks of the possibles is made somewhat grudgingly ; but that is because it really cannot be compared with rifles such as the ·375 magnum, ·400, or ·404 for all-round work, much less with the ·416 or ·425 for dangerous game exclusively ; and I am endeavouring to assist the beginner to choose a rifle which will give him the utmost possible satisfaction.

Another reason why the 10·75 mm. is so popular in Africa is undoubtedly due to its light weight : its low ballistics and comparatively low chamber pressure—low ballistics, that is, for a rifle of its calibre (·423)—permit of it being built very light. However, I do not recommend it : there are other infinitely more suitable and more satisfactory weapons ; why not choose one of them ?

·425 (*Westley Richards*)

Westley Richards builds his ·425 in double-barrelled as well as magazine form. Ballistically, as well as for all practical purposes of sport, there is really nothing to choose between this rifle and the ·416 save that the latter has a somewhat lower chamber pressure. Everything that I had to say with regard to the killing power and general efficiency of the ·416, can be equally applied to the ·425 ; as also can remarks concerning cost.

I can never understand why Westley Richards mounts a 28-inch barrel on the magazine edition of this rifle. The rifle was designed and intended for heavy and dangerous game ; such animals are not, or at any rate should not, be shot other than at close ranges : then why the long barrel ? It makes a most ungainly weapon of it for use in thick cover : as I have mentioned in the chapter dealing with elephant, I know a man who was nearly killed by a buffalo through having the muzzle of his 28-inch barrelled ·425 catch in something when he tried to turn round quickly to stop the charge. Of course, I am fully aware that Westley Richards will give you any length of barrel you like when building you a rifle or gun, but it occasionally happens that a man wants a rifle in a hurry, or wants a good second-hand one and has nobody capable of cutting down the barrel and resighting the weapon, and so must just take it as it is or leave it. I know of more than one man who was put off buying a ·425 on account of that long barrel : on three different occasions I have been offered a good second-hand ·425 magazine, but always turned it down ; though had it been fitted with a reasonably short barrel I would certainly have bought one of them.

I cannot think of the ·425-bore rifle without thinking of long barrels, and whenever I think of long barrels I am inevitably reminded of the remark made to me by one of the most experienced elephant hunters in Africa —a man who killed his thousandth elephant some considerable time ago. We were discussing elephant rifles when he gratuitously informed me that one could shoot more accurately with a long barrel than with a short one ! In view of the fact that we were discussing rifles suitable for elephant, and that we both knew very well the very close ranges at which elephant are shot, it struck me as being just about the most fatuous remark that a man of his experience could possibly have found to utter. I do not doubt that if you were shooting at 1,000 yards range you would find a 28-inch barrel more accurate than one of 24 inches ; but in spite of the fantastic ranges for which some rifles are ostensibly sighted, the fact remains that game are not shot at these long distances, and experience has shown that barrels of from 24 to 26 inches are as accurate as can ever be needed for all practical purposes of sport.

·440 (11·2 mm.) Mauser

As I have already mentioned in the chapter dealing with elephant rifles, the 11·2 mm. Mauser is not a suitable or satisfactory weapon for heavy, massive-boned animals owing to the very poor weight-to-diameter ratio of the bullet—even worse, much worse, than that of the 10·75 mm.—which means that it has practically no penetration at all.

In any case, I should never recommend it because the ammunition is only obtainable from Germany.

Rifles of larger bore than ·440 can hardly be considered as coming within the list of possible " all-round " rifles, so we need not discuss them here.

To sum up then :

For the sportsman who only wishes to use one rifle, the best and most suitable weapons are :—

Doubles : Holland's ·375 magnum ; Jeffery's ·400.

Magazines : Holland's ·375 magnum ; Jeffery's ·404.

(The 10·75 mm., provided it is built in England, could be used ; but I cannot recommend it.)

CHAPTER X

An Ideal Battery

THIS short chapter is written primarily for the benefit of the sportsman whose funds are limited, who wants everything that is essential, but nothing that is not absolutely necessary. The wealthy sportsman who can afford to indulge his fancy can have a battery of half a dozen or more rifles built for him if he wishes and therefore may skip this and leave it unread.

Now, since there are occasions on which a double is undoubtedly superior and definitely to be preferred to a magazine, and, by the same token, other occasions when the magazine is equally to be desired, no battery which does not include both types of weapon can possibly be considered as " ideal ". Personally, from my own experience, I am convinced that there is really only one type of shooting for which the magazine is to be preferred to any other type of action—even for the professional hunter : and that is when tackling more than two man-eating lions at night. In those parts of Africa in which most of my hunting takes place, lions, including man-eaters, almost invariably go about in threes—generally a male and two females—there are exceptions, of course, but three is the customary number. When tackling these at night, you will have a torch clamped on the rifle— the head-lamp is an abomination—which means that if you are using a double when you break the breech to reload after shooting two of the lions, the light will be directed towards the ground. You will, therefore, lose sight of the third lion and will not know what the brute is doing ; which is unpleasant when it is only perhaps 15 or 20 paces away. I am not sure that even a single-loader would not be preferable to a double in such circumstances, since with it you could at least keep the light shining directly towards the lions when reloading. For all other types of hunting I am sure that you will do just as well with a double as ever you will with a magazine. However, since a double is not essential other than for dangerous game at close quarters, and since I am writing this for the man who must consider the cost, a magazine must be included.

A double, then, throwing a 480- or 500-grain bullet we can take for granted. It only remains to decide on which of the magazines to choose to go with it. This is the customary battery : a heavy double for dangerous game, and a medium-bore magazine for general use. But which of all the various magazines is going to prove the most satisfactory and give the best results on the greatest possible number of occasions ? A battery of Rigby's splendid magazine rifles—such as a ·350 magnum for non-dangerous game and a ·416 for dangerous animals —with the double for use in thick cover—would, of course, constitute a magnificent battery. And if there was no such thing as an " all-round " rifle—that is, a weapon which is equally suitable for either soft-skinned or thick-skinned animals, dangerous or non-dangerous— then such a battery would undoubtedly be hard to beat.

But as we have seen in the preceding chapter, there is such a thing as an " all-round " rifle, and therefore a battery which includes a third weapon solely for use against non-dangerous animals, and which accordingly can only be considered in the light of a luxury, does not come up to the required specification—or rather it exceeds it, because it contains that which is not absolutely essential. Two rifles are all that is absolutely necessary ; and it is just a question of deciding on which of the " all-round " magazine rifles is to go with the double.

The choice, then, is limited to Jeffery's ·404 (when regulated for both standard and high-velocity ammunition) ; Holland's ·375 magnum ; and the 10·75 mm.

As I have already pointed out, the 10·75 mm. cannot be compared with either of the others because of its lack of penetration ; and so I am not going to consider it here since we are trying to find the weapon which will give the best results on all kinds of game under all conditions.

Of the other two : I have used them both, in conjunction with doubles and alone, with the greatest possible satisfaction. And although there is an appreciable difference in the weight of the blow delivered at close quarters, save in the most outrageously exceptional circumstances Holland's ·375 magnum is every bit as good as Jeffery's ·404. In fact, I am not sure that it is not every bit as good even in those " outrageously exceptional circumstances ", one of which I shall presently discuss ; and this, I think, is because its bullet seems to hold to a straighter course after penetrating an elephant's head, say, and this in turn appears to be on account of the excellent ratio of weight-to-diameter of the bullet in conjunction with its very high striking-velocity. But this is entering a realm which has never as yet been properly explored (other than by actual shooting—the *reason* for it all is still wrapped in mystery). But I do know that I have never yet had a solid bullet from the ·375 magnum break up or lose its direction ; whilst there are many cases on record of solid bullets fired from the ·404 doing curious things after entering an animal, including breaking up. (I have no recollection of ever hearing similar complaints concerning the ·400.)

However, since the weight of the blow inflicted at close quarters is the real deciding factor when it's a case of you knocking down the animal or his knocking you down —with probably worse to follow—whether or not that shot actually kills is of secondary importance : he can be killed later. Accordingly, for the benefit of the beginner, I shall just stick to what my " Knock-Out " blows tell us—whatever theory there may be in connection

with them, has been more than corroborated by actual
practice.   And since we are considering an " ideal ", no
contingency, no matter how remote, should be overlooked.
There is one which comes immediately to mind, for it is
by no means so remote as might be imagined.   It has
arisen with me on several occasions.

I am thinking of those occasions when you close a herd
of elephant or buffalo—but particularly elephant—in an
ocean of long grass, a great deal of which has been
trampled down, but with large, dense clumps still standing
here and there.   Now as so frequently happens, if the
herd has halted in a spot of this description, they will
have spread out in a rough horseshoe formation.   You
enter, as it were, between the prongs of the horseshoe.
You can see those in front of you up at the top of the
horseshoe and can hear the others on both sides of you,
but possibly cannot see them.   In all probability the
leaders of the herd will be up there in front of you, and
it will be at them naturally that you will be wanting to
open fire.

Now in very dense bush or close, heavy forest the
danger when in the centre of a herd of elephant is really
more apparent than real.   Because there is nearly always
a large tree or very dense bush, which even a herd of
stampeding elephant cannot stamp flat, behind which
you can shelter if a portion of the herd stampedes straight
towards you when you fire your first shot.   You can stand
there behind that friendly tree or bush in comparative
safety whilst the stampeding herd crashes past on both
sides of you.   But in long grass there is no such friendly
shelter ;   there is nothing which will cause the terrified
animals to deviate from their course.   They will come
through that grass like a squadron of battle-cruisers steam-
ing at full speed in line abreast—the only difference being
that those battle-cruisers would have a reasonable distance
between them, whereas elephant are gregarious beasts
and huddle together for moral support when frightened.

They will bunch together and be coming for you in a compact mass. So also, though to a slightly lesser extent, will buffalo. And either of them will be almost as irresistible as the battle-cruisers would be.

In a case of this description it is absolutely imperative that your rifle should have sufficient power to be able to be definitely relied upon to knock down an elephant. The mere capacity to turn him, alone, will not be sufficient. Because if the beasts are coming straight for you, you will naturally be firing at those in the centre of the line (if it is only the outside animals which are heading straight for you, you could dodge to one side), and there is no rifle on the market, there is no rifle that any man living could handle, which would have sufficient power to deliver such a tremendous blow that several elephant would be turned simultaneously by the one shot —you would need a field-gun to be capable of doing that. And if the rifle which you are using has only got enough power to turn a solitary elephant then, in a case of this sort, it would be little better than useless if you could not place the bullet in the animal's brain ; and conditions might very easily make that impossible. If the blow delivered is not sufficiently heavy to cause the elephant's legs to collapse under it, then the wretched beast may be utterly incapable of turning owing to the press of animals on either side.

Of course, in the great majority of cases, in somewhat similar circumstances, you would be opening fire with your double, but—and it all depends on how close those animals on either side of you are, and the extent to which the grass has been trampled down—you may consider it preferable to open fire with your magazine rifle. Because, if those animals on either side of you are very close, you may feel that should they take it into their heads to stampede towards you, you might not have time in which to reload the double before they were on you. And that would mean that had you fired one shot from the double, you would now have only one shot left with which to stop the stampede. The following incident, culled from Commander Blunt's *Elephant*, is most illustrative :

Blunt had closed a large herd of upwards of 80 elephant in an isolated patch of not-too-dense bush, with clumps of grass standing here and there. Having shot two or three of the herd, including the master bull, he found that the remainder of the herd had split up into the usual small family groups, and that he now had elephant all round him. He dropped another bull which was standing alone.

. . . next second a panic-stricken party of cows and calves came crashing through the bush on my left about six abreast and four deep. There was no evading them. . . . I just had time to blaze off a round, dropping one cow, but this did not stop them, so I fired my last cartridge and dropped another cow. This effectively checked the stampede, and they stood for some moments undecided which way to go. . . . My gunbearer and I " froze ", the distance between us and the leading elephant being only eight paces.

I could relate several other incidents of a like nature which have occurred in my own career, but they would be so very similar that I do not think that it is necessary to do so. Admittedly, one shot and one elephant down will frequently be sufficient to stop a stampede—but it very often will not. In fact, in my experience, I can definitely say that far, far more often than not the bringing down of one elephant alone will not be sufficient to stop the stampede—but two will. And that is the reason why it is sometimes—depending entirely on the conditions —desirable under such circumstances to open fire with your magazine rifle. (Let me repeat that this is for the benefit of the inexperienced man.)

But—and this is the point which I am endeavouring to make—it is also the reason why it is so absolutely essential that your magazine rifle should be one which will deliver a sufficiently heavy blow to enable you to rely upon it absolutely to knock down an elephant under all conditions wherein it could possibly, or reasonably, be expected to do so. And since amongst the definitely genuine " all-round " rifles there is only one which comes up to these requirements, then Jeffery's ·404 (when regulated for both standard and high-velocity ammunition) must be the magazine rifle to go with the double in our " ideal " battery—a battery consisting of everything that is essential and nothing that is not absolutely necessary, and yet wherein either rifle can be absolutely depended upon to satisfactorily answer any questions that you could ever be called upon to ask it.

To sum up then :

An ideal battery for the sportsman whose funds are limited consists of a best-quality double ·465 or ·470 non-ejector (or similar) and a Jeffery ·404 magazine regulated for both standard and high-velocity ammunition. (This, of course, if you expect to be doing a considerable amount of elephant hunting ; if not, but only a reasonable amount, then Holland's ·375 magnum will prove every bit as good—and probably would in any case.)

CHAPTER XI

Rifles for Small Game

THERE must be many men in Africa whose health, or the exigencies of whose life, will not permit them to indulge in big game hunting. But there is a type of hunting in which these men can indulge, and which will give them the greatest possible satisfaction, sport and pleasure, and withal, at little or no cost. All the joys of deer-stalking in Scotland and boar shooting in Spain or Morocco, without any of the expense and with no undue exertion—just sufficient, in fact, to compare with a round or two of golf.

In the vicinity of native villages herds of impala are frequently to be found like flocks of goats. Year in and year out they are to be found there. Reed-buck, bush-buck, klipspringer and duiker are also numerous in certain districts ; whilst warthog and bush-pig are classed along with baboons as vermin. In many districts these small buck can be shot without any licence being necessary other than your gun-permit. Warthog and bush-pig, of course, being vermin are always free, and give you some of the tastiest and juiciest meat in all Africa.

The pig and the baboons must do tens of thousands of pounds worth of damage every year throughout the length and breadth of the continent. You can have good fun —and be doing good work into the bargain—shooting these pests with a magnum small-bore.

You can spend many an enjoyable evening and many a happy weekend : just a gentle stroll round in the morning and another in the cool of the evening, a short and by no means difficult stalk, and you can consider yourself mighty unlucky if you do not get a shot on each occasion.

MAGNUM SMALL-BORE RIFLES

Rifle.	Weight of Bullet in grains.	Pressure in tons per square inch.	Velocity in ft. per sec.				Energy in ft.-lb.				Approximate Weight of Rifle in pounds.	
			Muzzle.	100 yd.	200 yd.	300 yd.	Muzzle.	100 yd.	200 yd.	300 yd.	D.B.	S.B.
·280 Halger . . .	100	22·5	3,800	3,480	3,160	2,840	3,210	2,690	2,220	1,790	—	10½
·280 ,, . . .	143	25·5	3,450	3,270	3,100	2,920	3,780	3,390	3,050	2,800	—	10½
·280 ,, . . .	180	24·5	3,000	2,860	2,720	2,580	3,600	3,270	2,960	2,670	—	10½
·280 Jeffery . . .	140	18·5	3,000	2,820	2,630	2,450	2,800	2,480	2,160	1,870	—	8½
·280	140	18·0	2,900	2,720	2,540	2,360	2,610	2,400	2,010	1,760	9½–10½	7½–9
·280	160	18·0	2,700	2,520	2,340	2,170	2,590	2,250	1,950	1,670	9½–10½	7½–9
·280	180	18·0	2,525	2,350	2,200	2,040	2,560	2,210	1,940	1,670	9½–10½	7½–9
·275 Magnum . .	160	18·0	2,700	2,550	2,380	2,230	2,590	2,310	2,010	1,780	9½–10	8–8½
·275 (7-mm. Rigby) .	140	19·0	2,750	2,580	2,400	2,230	2,360	2,070	1,800	1,550	—	7¼
·275 Rigby. . . .	140	17·0	2,650	2,500	2,330	2,160	2,220	1,950	1,690	1,450	8½	7½
·270 Winchester . .	130	21·0	3,100	2,890	2,680	2,470	2,770	2,410	2,080	1,760	—	7
·260 B.S.A. . . .	110	18·0	3,100	2,880	2,640	2,420	2,350	2,030	1,710	1,440	—	7½–8½
·256 Magnum Gibbs	145	19·5	2,600	2,440	2,280	2,120	2,180	1,920	1,670	1,450	—	7–7½
·256 (6·5-mm. Krag) .	135	21·5	2,800	2,620	2,450	2,270	2,350	2,060	1,800	1,530	—	7–8
·256 (6·5-mm. Mann. and Mann.-Schon.) .	135	17·5	2,600	2,430	2,250	2,080	2,030	1,770	1,520	1,300	—	7–8
·250 Savate . . .	87	19·0	3,000	2,710	2,420	2,150	1,720	1,410	1,130	890	—	7¼–7½
·246 Purdey . . .	100	18·0	2,950	2,750	2,550	2,350	1,940	1,680	1,450	1,230	9	—
·242 Vickers . . .	100	19·5	3,000	2,810	2,610	2,420	2,000	1,760	1,520	1,310	—	7
·240 Holland . . .	100	17·0	2,950	2,770	2,580	2,400	1,940	1,710	1,480	1,280	8	6¾–7

SMALL-BORE RIFLES

Rifle.	Weight of Bullet in grains.	Pressure in tons per square inch.	Velocity in ft. per sec.				Energy in ft.-lb.				Knock-Out Blow.	Approximate Weight of Rifle in pounds.
			Muzzle.	100 yd.	200 yd.	300 yd.	Muzzle.	100 yd.	200 yd.	300 yd.	Values.	S.B.
·275 (7 mm.) .	173	17·5	2,300	2,100	1,880	1,680	2,040	1,700	1,360	1,040	15·6	7
·256 (6·5 mm.) .	160	17·5	2,300	2,160	2,020	1,890	1,880	1,660	1,450	1,270	13·4	7–8

There is a splendid selection of magnum small-bores, which are ideal for this work, from which to choose. Of course, larger and more powerful weapons can be used perfectly satisfactorily ; but the man whom I have parti- cularly in mind will not be wanting to kill the larger species and, in all probability therefore, will not want to be bothered with a heavy rifle.

The high-velocity magnum small-bore, with its splendidly flat trajectory and high striking velocity, is undoubtedly the most satisfactory weapon for this sort of work. The ordinary small-bore is nothing like such a deadly weapon. If you shoot an animal like an impala in the heart with an ordinary small-bore, he will bound away at full speed and probably disappear in the grass. Owing to the very small entrance hole to the wound, there will be little or no blood spoor and the animal may get away altogether, possibly (if the bullet was not quite accurately placed in the heart) to die a miserable lingering death, or be pulled down and, quite literally, eaten alive by hyænas. Whereas, had a magnum been used, that same animal would have dropped stone dead in his tracks then and there. So that, apart altogether from your own satisfaction in making a clean kill, the magnum is decidedly a more humane weapon. Because, no matter what the animal is, the sportsman—if he deserves the title—should always endeavour to kill with the least possible infliction of pain, even if it is only a baboon.

In *Notes on Sporting Rifles* Major Burrard writes as follows :

The ordinary ·256, ·275, and ·303 small bores (not magnums) used to be favourite rifles with many. I have tried them all against game and do not like them. All three lack killing power. . . . One gooral I shot with a ·256 Mannlicher was hit three times before it could be caught and killed. All three shots were placed just behind the shoulder in a group which I could cover with the palm of my hand. Any one must have proved fatal in the end, but all three were not sufficient to kill, although they all seemed perfectly placed. . . .

The shock given to an animal when hit by a bullet travelling with an initial velocity of about 3,000 ft. per second is enormous, and seems to have a paralysing effect. I do not think the reasons for this are quite understood. I believe there is something in it more than mere bullet energy. When a M.V. of 2,500 f./s. is exceeded the blow of the impact seems to have a different effect on the tissues struck to the effect obtained with a bullet travelling at a lower speed. . . . Once an actual striking velocity of from 2,300 f./s. to 2,400 f./s. is exceeded, however, the killing effect seems to increase out of all proportion to any increase in bullet energy, even when there is no change in the weight of the bullet. . . . It is this peculiar property of shock which makes the magnum small bore such a splendid killing weapon, provided it is not abused by being employed against very heavy dangerous game at close quarters.

Now with regard to the choice of a rifle : I do not know if it would be wise to recommend rifles in the ·240–·260-bore group. These little rifles were principally designed for deer-stalking in Scotland and similar work ; and I understand are also used with great satisfaction for boar shooting in Austria, Spain, Morocco and other countries. I have never shot boar in either Austria or Spain, and have no means of knowing how an Austrian or Spanish boar compares with an African warthog from the point of view of weight, bulk and thickness of hide ; but a full-grown African warthog is a pretty massive brute with, for his size, a fairly tough hide. I do not know whether or not the light 100-grain bullets with their tremendously high striking velocity at all ranges might perhaps tend to blow to pieces on striking a warthog's head or shoulder (there is no doubt that they would prove eminently suitable for all the other animals mentioned in this chapter), though I hardly think they would. However, never having used the 100-grain bullet myself, I prefer to play for safety and suggest that if you are contemplating a ·240 or similar rifle you should first try and find out how it is likely to behave on a warthog— if nobody else can tell you, your gunsmith almost certainly will be able to and his advice will be well worth following : it will naturally be to his benefit to sell you the weapon

9

which he has reason to believe will give you the greatest satisfaction ; it makes no difference to him whether it is a ·240 or a ·300—the price of both rifles is the same, he makes a similar profit from either.

But although I have not as yet had an opportunity of trying out the 100-grain bullet, I can speak from personal experience of bullets ranging upwards from 140 grains and can definitely state that they will be found most deadly. I do not care for the copper-pointed bullets as I find that if they fail to strike any bone larger than a rib they are very apt to slip right through like a solid to possibly wound another member of the herd standing beyond the one at which I have fired ; I find the semi-pointed soft-nose much more reliable.

In this type of shooting anything over 200 yards may be considered a very long shot, whilst ranges running upwards of 250 yards need hardly be considered. The average range will probably be found to vary between 75 and 175 yards.

I have frequently heard men argue that the cost of magnum small-bores and their ammunition was excessive, and that for shooting these small animals an ordinary ·256, ·275, or ·303 was quite good enough. Now it has already, I trust, been made clear that the ordinary small-bore is not always " good enough " ; but apart from that, even if the rifle does cost more, surely any man will derive infinitely greater pleasure and satisfaction from using a really well built and nicely finished weapon than from using a cheap, mass-production affair—to say nothing of the greater certainty of absolute accuracy.

Then, with regard to the cost of the ammunition : admittedly the ammunition for a magnum costs anything up to nearly double that of ordinary small bore cartridges, but then the very much flatter trajectory of the high-velocity bullet will mean a great many more clean kills, particularly at the longer ranges, both because it is not necessary to have to estimate the distance—as is absolutely

essential with a low-velocity weapon owing to the comparatively small margin of error that is permissible with
these small animals—and also because far more often
than not the one shot will be sufficient where, as in Major
Burrard's case just quoted, two, three, or possibly even
more, shots may have to be fired with an ordinary small
bore. Obviously, therefore, since you will probably not
fire more than half the number of cartridges, if so many,
the difference in the cost of the ammunition need not be
considered—unless it is to show that the magnum
ammunition will probably work out cheaper than the
ordinary.

Let me assure anybody who has not tried this type of
shooting that it is to be most thoroughly recommended
provided that suitable rifles are used. And the magnum
small bore is undoubtedly the most suitable weapon.

MINIATURE RIFLES

In Africa, the vast majority of men used to use a
shot-gun for birds, etc., for the pot. But it was found
that a shot-gun made too much noise, particularly if one
was hoping for elephant. As a result, most men nowadays
use a miniature rifle for this purpose. Provided
that it is not larger than ·295-bore, it makes no noise at
all—at least, nothing worth considering ; and affords
you endless pleasure and enjoyment at little or no cost.

The principal miniature rifles (usually known as Rook
or Rabbit rifles) are : ·380, ·360 No.5, ·320, ·310 Greener,
·300 Sherwood, ·300 or ·295 (the cartridges are the same),
·255 Jeffery, ·297/·250, ·297/·230 Morris Tube, ·22
Hornet, ·22 hi-power Savage, ·22 rim-fire. The only 4 of
these of which I have had any personal experience are the
·295, the ·255 Jeffery, the ·22 Savage, and the ·22 rim-
fire. Prior to the introduction of the modern high-
velocity non-fouling ·22 rim-fire and the ·22 Hornet, I
used to consider that the ·255 Jeffery was easily the best
of them. From all accounts the Hornet is a wonderful

little weapon ; but I have never had an opportunity of trying it.   The new high-velocity ·22 rim-fire is probably the best because of its non-fouling ammunition :   you needn't bother about cleaning it after firing—an immense asset—whilst it is just about as powerful at 100 yards as the old cartridge was at the muzzle.   Needless to say, a telescope sight should always be used ;   and even a 'scope-sighted miniature rifle will be found to cost no more than a low-priced shot-gun, whilst the ammunition for the ·22 rim-fire costs next to nothing and is excellent for keeping your eye in if you are not constantly hunting.

CHAPTER XII

Sights, Sighting and Trajectories

IF you are to obtain the greatest satisfaction from your rifles and do the best work with them, it is imperative that they should be fitted with the most suitable type of sight for that work. And not only that, but that the sights should be suitable for you. Everybody knows that if the rifle is to fit you perfectly it should be built to your measurements, just like a suit of clothes ; but they frequently forget the fact that your eyesight can differ from the next man's just as much as can your physique.

When aiming over the open sights, the eye is given the extremely difficult task of attempting to focus three different objects, all at different distances, at one and the same time : the backsight, the foresight, and the object at which you are aiming. Now the eye has an astonishing depth of focus, but there are limits to what it can do ; and these limits vary with different individuals. Of course, no man's eye can bring all three objects into definite focus simultaneously ; and the greater the distance between the three objects, the more difficult the attempt.

From this it will be seen that the closer the backsight is brought to the breech, the harder the task set the eye and, therefore, the greater the strain on that eye—apart from the fact that the backsight will appear even more blurred than it need do. Of course, there is a limit to the distance at which it can be mounted away from the eye ; because, as it is moved towards the muzzle, the sight-base—i.e. the distance between foresight and backsight—is reduced, and a very short sightbase permits inaccuracies to creep in when shooting at the longer ranges. But since it is very much easier to aim correctly when both sights can be seen with a reasonable degree of clearness, it is far better to have the backsight mounted a trifle too far from the eye rather than a trifle too close, particularly when the comparatively short ranges at which game are shot in Africa is borne in mind. Theory is all very well, but it is what actually happens in the field that matters to the practical sportsman ; and it actually happens that no matter how long the sightbase no man can shoot accurately with a rifle on which the backsight is merely an indistinguishable blurr, but that he can shoot as accurately as could ever be needed in practical sport when he can see his backsight clearly even though the sightbase is a comparatively short one.

There are one or two outstanding exceptions, all the more noticeable because these are so rare, but speaking generally and judging from the manner in which they sight their rifles, one might well be excused for believing that gunsmiths as a whole have not the remotest conception of the requirements of a sporting rifle from the point of view of its sighting arrangements. And save for the most experienced, the men who buy these rifles apparently never give a thought to such matters but are satisfied to take the weapons just as the gunsmiths supply them : hence a lot of the bad shooting one sees.

You can quite easily determine for yourself the most suitable distance for the backsight by cutting an imitation backsight out of anything at all—tin, cardboard or something of the sort—place this on your rifle or shot-gun and aim over it at some fairly distant object ; then move it about until you can see it clearly in conjunction with the foresight. All that is then necessary is to mark that spot and measure the distance thence to the heel of the butt. When having a new rifle built or when buying a second-hand weapon, if you give this measurement to your gunsmith you can always have the backsight mounted the same distance from your eye—the distance which you have found to be the most suitable for you—on any type of weapon, double, single or magazine. Occasionally, of course, on certain types of magazine rifles when bought secondhand it may not be possible to have any very great alteration made owing to the design of the backsight mounting ; but because of the long bolt action it is seldom that one finds the backsight too close to the eye on this type of weapon. But it can always be done on doubles, and generally can on magazines, and is always well worth while.

Never attempt to fire a shot at game without first testing your rifle at a target. And important and all as this test is even with a new rifle, it is ten times more so in the case of a second-hand weapon. Even the very best firms, although they may have built you a brand new rifle to your own measurements and your own specification, will nevertheless invariably recommend you to try it at a target to make absolutely sure that the sights are suitable and as you want them. The importance of this test cannot be too strongly emphasized, though it is all too frequently overlooked. I am sure that it is no exaggeration to say that there must be hundreds of animals wounded in Africa every year through this test not having been made. And if it is important in the case of a rifle which will be principally used on non-dangerous animals, how much more important must it be in the case of a weapon which is intended solely for use against dangerous game at very close quarters. Yet although I have occasionally seen a man test a medium- or small-bore magazine rifle, I can honestly state that I have never yet seen a man in Africa test a large-bore double-barrel weapon. They have invariably made the same remark —though not, perhaps, in the same words—to the effect that the ammunition was far too expensive (it costs anything from 2s. to 2s. 6d. a shot landed out here) and that they saw no fun in throwing away five or ten bob by blowing a few holes in a piece of paper ! It apparently did not occur to them that they were valuing their lives at less than half a sovereign.

FORESIGHTS

The bead pattern is out and away the best type of foresight for sporting purposes. For general African use it should not be too fine, because of the size of the animals and the comparatively short ranges at which they are shot. Personally for my medium-bore rifle I like a medium bead. (Of course, if you are contemplating a small-bore for shooting the smaller varieties of game, then a fine or fine-to-medium bead will be the best and most suitable—the size, of course, must depend on the eyesight of the man behind the rifle—but, for small animals, the bead should be as fine as the eyesight will permit with ease. If the bead is a fine one it should be slightly undercut so that its own shadow will cause it to stand out clearly from the stem in all lights.) For my heavy double, which is only used at very close ranges, I use a large bead. Because the closer the animal is to you the larger he appears, and therefore the less likelihood of the bead blocking out too much of him as would happen if a very large bead was used for small animals at long ranges. A large bead can be seen more easily and picked up far more quickly in the event of a snap-shot being necessary—particularly in the dense black shade in heavy forest wherein the light is frequently none too good. The foresights generally fitted on powerful rifles are much too small for the work for which these weapons are intended, and for the conditions under which they are mostly used.

Ivory-tipped foresights are delightful to use—so long as the ivory tip stays " put " ; but in my experience they are not very durable : sooner or later your second gun-bearer will stand the rifle carelessly or roughly against a tree, and the next thing is that you are minus an ivory tip. Even if this does not happen, the ivory shrinks in the heat and eventually drops out of its own accord ; and it goes without saying that it inevitably does so when you are actually hunting and without you or anyone else noticing until you try to take a shot and find yourself with only half a foresight.

I believe that both Parker's and Marble's ivory and gold foresights are excellent, but I have never used one myself. For years I always had my foresights tipped with platina. This can be fused on to metal and therefore cannot drop off. Further, I used to dab a little white foresight paint on the bead of the rifle I habitually used in heavy forest, so that I had all the advantages of ivory-tipped sights without any of their disadvantages. If the paint managed to get rubbed off when I was out for a few days without my reserve supply, well—the platina was there and was perfectly satisfactory. However, I decided that the paint business was a bit of a nuisance, and thought that I would try enamel-tipped sights. I find these just about ideal, and although I have heard that they are not too durable that certainly has not been my experience : they seem to be everlasting, and are a delight to use.

A folding " moon " nightsight, which can be fitted to any rifle, is a great help when tackling marauding elephant and buffalo at night. But be sure and test it at a target in daylight to satisfy yourself that its elevation is all right. It can, of course, be used in heavy forest in the daytime if the ordinary sight is not showing up too well ; but it is not really suitable for such work as it can be accidentally pushed down all too easily when forcing your way through thick cover.

A spare foresight, identical with that on the barrel, should always be carried in a trap let into the base of the grip on each and all of your rifles. There is then no fear of it being lost or damaged, yet it is always at hand should you be unfortunate enough to need it when out hunting. I must admit that in spite of the amount of use that my rifles get—and it is inevitable that when hunting twelve months a year they will from time to time be subjected to a certain amount of rough handling—I have never yet had to fit a spare foresight when out hunting. Yet, since there is no telling when it *may* be required, I invariably have a spare foresight in the trap in the pistol grip on all my rifles.   Therein it acts as insurance, if nothing else—for, with the customary contrariness of things, if I had not got a spare sight then nothing is surer than the fact that I should be needing one, and needing it badly.

A good foresight protector is also a most necessary article : though for years I was without and never needed one, I was never really happy until I had them.   Westley Richards's special folding pattern is undoubtedly the best ; though Holland also makes quite a good one.   The great advantage of these two is that they are always on the rifles and consequently always there when you want to stand the weapons against a tree or rock ; the removable types have to be hunted and fumbled for and are all too easily lost.

OPEN BACKSIGHTS

There are two types of open backsight which can be fitted to sporting rifles : the V and the U ; and of these the V is far and away the better and is almost invariably fitted to British rifles.   Without exception, every Continental-built rifle that I have ever seen in Africa has been fitted with a U backsight.   To my mind this pattern is utterly unsuitable for sporting purposes : it is slow and tends greatly to blur.   But you should insist on the V being broad and shallow, because this allows of a much quicker aim being taken and gives you a good view of your target.   The deep, narrow V or notch that one so frequently sees is, in my opinion, a ghastly mistake : it blocks out far too much of the animal.   The combination so beloved of gunsmiths—i.e. this deep, narrow V used in conjunction with an almost microscopically minute bead on the foresight—even on powerful D.B. rifles, is hopeless, quite hopeless : the tiny bead is practically invisible in anything but the most open country (where such a rifle would not be required) as it nestles away down at the bottom of that deep cleft, whilst the shoulders of the V blot out the entire countryside ; if you are endeavouring to take a shot at a big black animal standing in dense shadow with sights of this description, it is sheer luck if you succeed in killing him, because the shoulders of the V will completely prevent you from seeing if he moves the instant before you press the trigger.

The standard should slope towards the muzzle so that it will catch the light—what little light there is—when in heavy forest. If you are told that this will cause it to dazzle you when in open country, that will be true if the sun happens to be in a certain position behind you ; but then there is no need to use an open sight in open country : you should be using either an aperture sight or a telescope sight—but I will come to that anon. If the backsight is made either vertical or sloping towards the breech you will be unable to see it in a bad light or when aiming at a dark-coloured animal standing in heavy shadow : you will have to lower the muzzles so that the foresight disappears and then raise them again so as to be sure that you are taking the whole bead and nothing but the bead, just as when shooting at night with the aid of a torch—save that at night the backsight is seen in silhouette, which helps slightly, but by day it is not even silhouetted—it merges entirely into the background. This is much too slow when tackling the big fellows at close quarters in thick cover. But if the backsight can be seen instantly on raising the rifle, it helps enormously in taking a quick shot. Since most of your shooting with the big rifle will take place in thick and fairly thick cover, it is surely the part of wisdom to have it sighted in the most suitable manner for that type of work ? It will not by any means dazzle you every time you use it in more open country—only very occasionally when the sun catches it over your shoulder ; and I am convinced from my own experience that these occasions are so very few and far between that they are more, far more, than offset by the vastly greater number of occasions in thick cover when the sight sloping towards the muzzles will be of the greatest possible assistance to you. The men who recommend that the backsight should slope towards the breech are those who have done practically all their shooting in very open country ; if you are going to use open sights for that type of shooting, then it would undoubtedly be preferable to have the sight made as they suggest on the rifle which you intend using for that particular purpose, but not for your big game weapon.

Too many men are apt to generalize on the question of sighting, apparently assuming that what is suitable for one type of shooting must be equally suitable for another, indeed every other, type with, perhaps, just a small variation in the size of the foresight. There could be no greater mistake : the rifle you require for use in thick cover is an entirely different weapon from that which you would want for use in open country : the conditions under which it will be used are entirely different ; is it then to be wondered at, or considered unreasonable, that it should require entirely different sighting ?

The standard sight should stand alone : there should be no additional leaves fitted. If you have a number of leaf sights fitted, ostensibly marked for all sorts of fantastic ranges at which no man in his right mind would ever even dream of shooting game, you will be greatly tempted to use them, and if you do you will inevitably find yourself missing through having overestimated the range. Have your standard sight set for the longest range possible —that is, wherein the bullet does not rise unduly high at any intermediate range—study the trajectory curve of your rifle, and just aim a trifle higher at the longer ranges than you normally would. You will find this method

by far the most satisfactory and certain, particularly
when using modern rifles. The thought of studying the
trajectory curve of your rifle may seem at first glance to
be a frightfully technical and difficult proposition. But
in actual fact it is only a question of memorizing one,
or at the very most two, numbers : the amount by which
the bullet drops at 250 yards and again, possibly, at
300 yards. But you will so rarely shoot beyond 250 yards
—though you may think that you are !—that I am quite
certain that it will be found perfectly satisfactory to just
memorize the bullet-drop at 250 yards and if the animal
appears to be that distance away from you, just aim *half*
that amount higher than you would aim at closer ranges.
I suggest half the amount of bullet-drop because the
animal in all probability is not as far away as he seems
to be.

For example : If you are carrying a ·350 magnum
sighted for 175 yards and see an animal standing at
apparently 250 yards and you cannot get closer, then
instead of fiddling about with sights you will just aim
3½ inches higher than you normally would at an animal
standing at, say, 150 yards. This because a ·350 magnum which is sighted for 175 yards will show a bullet-
drop of just under 7 inches at 250 yards. And since it
is absurd to speak of half *inches* when considering ranges
of 250 *yards*, this simply means that you will aim a trifle
higher on the animal's shoulder than you would at a
closer range. So actually you have nothing to remember
at all, though it is a good plan to try to remember the
bullet-drop at 250 yards and possibly at 300 yards just
at first, because this helps to give you a mental picture of
what is happening to the bullet after it has left the muzzle.
And if you once get hold of this mental picture there will
be no fear of you missing through sending your bullet
over the animal's back. At all ranges under 200 yards
you have nothing to worry about, because the bullet does
not rise more than about 2½ inches above the line of sight

at the highest point of its trajectory curve. As far as your heavy rifle is concerned, you have nothing to remember because it is only for use at close quarters, and in any case will comfortably stand sighting for 150 yards—which will give you a flat trajectory up to about 170 yards since the bullet will have only dropped about 2½ inches by the time it gets there—and there is not one chance in a thousand that you will be wanting to use it at longer ranges than that ; in fact, you will seldom if ever use it at more than 100 yards.

If you have your rifle covered with those fascinating little leaf sights and see an animal standing, you think, nearer 300 yards than 200 yards what could be easier then to flip up that 300-yard leaf and have your bullet whizz over the animal's back ? Haven't I done it myself ? Haven't we all done it in days gone by before we learnt sense ? The animal was probably only 200 yards away after all. But with the method of sighting which I recommend your bullet would not have missed him : it would simply have taken him somewhat higher on the shoulder than usual, that's all.

All sporting rifles are regulated and shot and have their sights adjusted at 100 yards range. Animals are not sufficiently obliging to measure off the distance they stand from you in round figures ; so there is really nothing to be gained in having a rifle most carefully sighted for some such distance as, say, 175 yards. In the trajectory tables which I have given at the end of this chapter, I show the trajectory curves of various rifles sighted for 175 yards. I have done so because, as I mentioned in the preface, I have taken these tables with the Author's generous permission from *Notes on Sporting Rifles*, and Major Burrard believes in being very accurate. Also, it enables a man to get a very excellent idea of the actual curve followed by his bullet. But in actual practice, by far the handiest way is to just tell your gunsmith to take the " six o'clock " aim on a 4–inch bull at 100 yards and have the rifle group centrally, or a trifle higher than centrally, but not lower, in the bull. This will give you a bullet-rise of a trifle over 2 inches at this convenient range ; and this in turn will give you as flat a trajectory as you are ever likely to require in Africa, or, indeed, anywhere else, with modern rifles.

At first glance it may appear that these tables hopelessly complicate matters ; but remember, few men, other than professional hunters, have more than two rifles, and even professional hunters will only have rifles in certain groups, and all the rifles in those groups have, for all practical purposes, identical trajectories. Besides, as I have pointed out, the heavy rifles are only used at close ranges, so that it is not necessary to bother about their trajectory curves if they are sighted as I suggest. The only reason I have included these tables is because I think that they may help the inexperienced man to get an idea of the curve followed by any particular bullet.

Although I have been talking about shots at 250 yards range, it must not be imagined that many shots are taken at that distance. I only choose it because it is about the maximum range at which you will ever be called upon to shoot in Africa, and because it is really the only range for which it might be desirable to memorize the drop of your bullet. I have also chosen to discuss aiming at the shoulder because it is the largest and most vulnerable target : shooting at game is a very different thing from shooting at a target. When on the range you may consider a 6-inch circle as a fairly generous-sized bull at 250 yards ; but on the range you can make yourself as comfortable as you like : you are not fatigued, nor hungry, nor thirsty, nor suffering perhaps from the heat. You will be able to place your shots very much more accurately on the target than you could in the Bush, when you may be called upon to fire from an impossibly uncomfortable position at an animal which may disappear at any moment. And it is for this reason that precious few men attempt to shoot an animal between the eyes at any but the closest ranges.

One frequently hears men tell how they took a " very full sight " or a " very fine sight " as the case may be at some particular range, and some gunsmiths actually recommend this method of aiming in their catalogues. Now surely this is the most impossible method of aiming : since it is admittedly extremely difficult to estimate the range correctly to within 50 or 75 yards, then how can anybody hope to be able to estimate the correct amount of foresight to take when the smallest fraction of an inch will throw the bullet hopelessly out ?   The whole object of the bead foresight is to assist and enable the shooter to take the same amount of foresight always : the bead, the whole bead and nothing but the bead.   It is far easier to learn the amount by which your bullet drops at 250 yards and remember that, than to learn the correct amount of foresight to take, since at the best it can only be a matter of guesswork, and mighty difficult guesswork at that.   Besides, you have two guesses to make instead of only one : first you have to guess the correct range and then guess the correct amount of foresight to take for this distance.   Whereas, with my method of sighting you have nothing to guess at all since you will have, for all practical purposes, a flat trajectory for all ranges up to and including 250 yards with a modern medium-bore rifle in the magnum group (and, of course, the same applies to the magnum small-bores).

APERTURE BACKSIGHTS

It is amazing how seldom one sees an aperture sight being used.   Here on the Zambezi, where I have been hunting for years, I can only remember seeing one other man apart from myself using a peepsight.   The average sportsman in Africa, if he has heard of a peep-sight at all, invariably associates it with target work and imagines that it is not suitable for any other purpose.

No greater mistake could be made; for the peepsight is out and away the best and quickest type of backsight that there is.

Of course, when a peepsight is used on a rifle, the open backsight should be made so as to fold down. If this is not done you lose all the advantages of the aperture sight. That only other man who used a peepsight, to whom I have just referred, complained that he found it much too slow and had given up trying to use it. I expected to find that either the aperture was too small or else that he was trying to use it in conjunction with a standard backsight: and that was exactly what he was trying to do. The aperture was all right, though somewhat smaller than I should have liked; but he had a standard backsight which could not be folded down. He was astonished when I told him that a peepsight should be used alone with the foresight—he didn't believe it possible to do so; but since there wasn't a gunsmith within hundreds of miles, what would I recommend him to do about it? As he had another rifle for use in thick cover, I suggested that he remove the open sight altogether from this one. We did that; and as there happened to be a croc. lying on a sandbank just across from where we were sitting, I told him not to bother about his peepsight or attempt to look at it but just place his foresight on the spot in which he wished to put his bullet and squeeze the trigger. He fired; the croc. gave a convulsive jump and lay quivering, dead as a kippered herring; and my companion was at that moment, I think, the happiest and proudest man in all Africa.

Gunsmiths are greatly to blame for this incorrect method of sighting rifles: again and again have I seen rifles in their showrooms fitted with aperture sights and standard backsights; one sees the same weapons illustrated in their catalogues. They do not appear to realize how utterly useless such a combination is for any kind of sporting purpose; nor, unless the sportsman definitely orders a folding backsight, does it occur to them to point out that such a sight is absolutely essential when a peep-sight is being used. There are, of course, a few exceptions—but they are precious few.

When the open sight is made so as to fold down, a small, strong bolt or slide should be fitted which will definitely hold it up and prevent any possibility of it being pushed down accidentally when forcing a way through thick cover, should it be found necessary to use it. But this is quite a simple matter. The usual spring is not sufficient, though it should also be there to keep the sight down when not in use.

The correct method of using the aperture sight is not to think of, or worry about it, at all—and do not attempt to look *at* it—look *through* it. Just throw the rifle to your shoulder, place the bead of the foresight on the spot that you wish to hit, and press the trigger. Nothing could be simpler or quicker. Any man's eye naturally and instinctively looks through the centre of a hole; do not bother your head about centring the foresight—it will do that of its own accord.

The beauty of a peepsight is that you get a perfectly clear view of the animal at which you are aiming—just as you do with a telescope sight—which is a tremendous advantage where running shots are concerned; but no small advantage at any time, because there is no possibility of " taking too much foresight ". Since you have only to think of the foresight, it is vastly quicker than the open sight. And further, since when using the open sight everything which comes below the level of the standard is blocked out, you only see at the most half of the picture, so that you may find it extremely difficult to place your shot accurately in a small animal at long range, particularly if the animal's body happens to be partially concealed by bush or grass; but with the peepsight you will get a clear view of everything that there is to be seen.

The additional advantages of the aperture sight are the saving in eye-strain, since you have only two objects to focus instead of three ; and the appreciably greater accuracy which must ensue from the very much longer sight base—nearly double that available when open sights are used. In fact, I have heard a well-known expert give it as his considered opinion that a properly designed and properly mounted aperture sight practically doubled the accuracy with which you could shoot, and reduced by fully half the time required in which to aim. And I fully agree with him.

Always use the largest possible aperture ; it gives you a larger field of view and permits more light to come through. At first you may imagine that accurate shooting is an impossibility with such a colossal hole as it will appear to be ; but do not *try* to centre the foresight, do not think of the matter or of the size of the aperture ; confidence will come after you have fired a shot or two and realized how easy it is.

The disadvantages of a peepsight are that it cannot be used in a very bad light and that the peepsight as fitted to a double rifle cannot be carried ready for instant use when hunting on foot, owing to its liability to catch in things and become festooned with grass, trailing vines or something of the sort, if not bent or pushed down in all probability at the very instant that you want to use it. Accordingly, since all hunting is conducted on foot in Africa—one does not refer to those alleged sportsmen who chase game in motor-cars—your double rifle should be fitted with a single standard sight only. But you should always have a large apertured peepsight mounted on the tail end of the bolt of all your magazine rifles. In fact, I cannot understand why gunsmiths do not mount peepsights as standard fittings on all magazine rifles, just as much as ordinary open sights. It is merely a case of educating the sporting public into the way of thinking in terms of peepsights ; no man who has used a good and

properly designed aperture sight would willingly return
to the open sight.   Until you have used one, you can
have no idea of the quickness of the peepsight : the rapidity with which you can get your shot off with accuracy is
astonishing—so much so, in fact, that I am not sure that
a really well-built, well-balanced magazine rifle fitted
with a reasonably short barrel and carrying a properly
designed peepsight with a large aperture on Holland's
latest type of mounting could not be fired (I am assuming
that it is being carried all ready for instant use, as when
following up a wounded lion) if not quite, then very,
very nearly as quickly as a double fitted with open sights.

At the present moment my battery for dangerous game
consists of a Holland double ·465 " Royal " and a Rigby
·416 magazine.   The double is fitted with a single standard backsight, whilst the magazine has an aperture
sight.   Now were I told that I must discard one or other
of those rifles, and in future use one and one only for all
conditions—I sometimes wonder what I would do : much
and all as I should hate to part with my " Royal ", that
peepsight is mighty attractive.   I dare say if it actually
came to the pinch I would not hesitate, but would stick
to my double ; but the very fact that I find some small
difficulty in answering the question now when the necessity for doing so is not forced upon me—the very fact that
I spare a thought for it at all, or admit to any hesitation in
answering—may perhaps, bearing in mind how essentially
staunch an upholder I am of the double-barrelled rifle,
serve to indicate something of the tremendous importance
that I attach to the aperture sight.

With the aperture sight you can allow for the bullet-
drop at long ranges in exactly the same way as with the
open sights (or telescope sight, for that matter).   In
fact, you can do so with a far greater degree of accuracy,
particularly when aiming at a small animal, since you can
see the whole animal and not only the upper part of his
body, which is all that you could see when aiming over

the open sights, and consequently a more accurate estimate of the allowance by which you are aiming higher
can be made.

TELESCOPE SIGHTS

There is an oft-repeated cry heard, not only in Africa
but throughout the big game hunting world, whenever
telescope sights are mentioned—generally by those who
do not possess one !—that telescope sights are unsporting :
not fair on the game. How *can* they be considered
" unsporting ", or " not fair on the game " ?   Is it fairer
to an animal to drop him stone dead where he stands with
an accurately placed bullet, or to fire a badly-aimed shot
which will only wound him and give him hours, or
possibly even days, of misery and pain followed perhaps
by a beastly death—sometimes, quite literally, eaten alive
by hyænas ?

It is acknowledged to be the essence of unsportsmanlike
behaviour to needlessly wound an animal—as, for instance, those, I am sorry to say by no means unknown,
occasions when men have deliberately crippled animals
such as elephant—animals, that is, that cannot get away
on three legs—for the sole purpose of obtaining a good
close-up photograph of him apparently unwounded.   It
is acknowledged to be equally unsportsmanlike to just
stand by and watch some wretched beast dying and not
put him out of his misery with the greatest possible dis-
patch.   In other words the true sportsman kills his beast
with the least possible infliction of pain and suffering.
And since telescope sights indubitably assist you to an
enormous extent to place your bullet accurately—which
means a more instantaneous death to the animal—how
can they possibly be considered " unsporting " ?

If that argument was to be followed up, then high-
velocity rifles must be equally " unsporting "—in fact,
to run the thing to its logical conclusion, even bows and
arrows must be " unsporting ", since they enable the

hunter to kill from afar.   Knives and clubs, which would necessitate the hunter coming to actual grips with his quarry, could be the only truly " sporting " weapons ! But this, of course, is ridiculous.

A telescope sight can be a tremendous asset, not only for long shots, but when an animal is partially concealed behind bush or grass.   It is also of incalculable benefit when the light is bad ; it can be used, and effective aim taken, when the ordinary sights cannot be seen at all. From two to three magnifications will be found to be ample. These comparatively low powers give a much larger field of view and very much greater luminosity—a low-powdered 'scope sight can be used most effectively for occasional nightwork.

The disadvantages of a telescope sight usually put forward are, that it spoils the balance of a rifle ; that it adds to the weight of a rifle ; that, being a delicate optical instrument, it is far too easily damaged ; that it is too expensive ; that it is slow ; and that it is a liability when facing a charging animal such as a lion.

Now these indictments are almost invariably put forward by men whose hunting days are over and who are thinking of the 'scope sights they saw and possibly used anything up to fifty years ago, or by men who have only used cheap 'scopes cheaply mounted or else 'scopes that were incorrectly mounted, and have never used modern 'scopes properly mounted in modern mounts. Of recent years there have been enormous improvements not only in the telescopes themselves, but also in the method of mounting 'scope sights.

Let us take these indictments in turn :

It depends entirely on how a telescope is mounted whether or not it spoils the balance of the rifle—it may improve it.   If the telescope is to be a more or less per-manent fitting on the rifle, the balance can be checked after it has been mounted ; if it is of the quickly-detach-able variety for occasional use it really does not matter a whole lot if it does slightly upset the balance, because you will only be using it for deliberate shots—besides, as I have stated, it need not necessarily upset the balance at all.

That a 'scope sight adds to the weight of a rifle is indisputable. But rifles *can* be built considerably lighter than they usually are : there is nothing to prevent you having one of these special light models built for you which, with 'scope sight mounted, will be little if any heavier than the normal weight of that rifle fitted with open sights. (The reason why rifles are usually built somewhat heavier than they need be built is because some men are more sensitive to recoil than others and might find the recoil of the lighter model unpleasant : this reduction in weight with corresponding increase in the severity of the recoil is overcome by the weight of the telescope and its mounts.) If you do not want a special light rifle, because you expect to be using the rifle principally with open sights and the telescope only occasionally, I should consider that the additional weight of the telescope when mounted would be an asset, because it would enable the rifle to settle down more steadily in your hand when aiming ; if you are only using it now and then there is no necessity for you to carry it on the rifle : with modern mounts it can be attached to, or removed from, the rifle in a matter of two seconds or so without any tools whatsoever being required—why not carry it in its holster ?

A telescope sight is indisputably an optical instrument ; but I certainly cannot agree that a modern high-quality 'scope sight is delicate. It will stand up to considerably more knocking about than any ordinary foresight. It is astonishing just how much punishment a good 'scope sight will take without suffering. I hunt all the year round, in all weathers and at all seasons ; I have used 'scope sights for years with the utmost satisfaction ; nor, in spite of many knocks and falls—practically inevitable

in the life I live—have I ever had a 'scope sight injured
or show the slightest falling off in accuracy after one of
these little adventures.   It is frequently said that the man
who hands a 'scope-sighted rifle to a native gunbearer to
carry will not long enjoy the benefits of a telescope sight.
That is certainly not my experience.   In all the years I
have hunted I have never seen a boy of mine knock over
a rifle of mine or drop it carelessly in a manner which I
should consider worthy of reprimand.   Whenever a rifle
of mine has been knocked over I have, myself, been
the guilty party : stand the rifle against a tree, sit down
with my back towards the tree, forget about the rifle,
put my hand round to get a handkerchief or a cigarette-
case out of my hip pocket, and have my elbow send the
rifle clattering.   My experience is that the native, not
being accustomed to many possessions, is extremely
careful of anything of yours that you may hand him to
look after—far more so than you, yourself, would be of
that particular article.   Of course, if you are in the habit
of throwing your rifles about, you would be well advised
to only have a quickly-detachable 'scope :· you can then
remove it before testing your skill as a rifle thrower.
But as far as the ordinary individual is concerned, I can
see no reason whatever why a modern high-quality 'scope
sight should not last a lifetime.

The initial cost of a good 'scope sight is undoubtedly
high, though it is frequently the mounting that costs the
money—sometimes as much as the 'scope itself (when
gunmakers quote you the price of a 'scope sight, the price
includes the cost of fitting and regulating).   However, I
am perfectly convinced—again speaking from my own
experience—that the cost is covered over and over again
by the intense pleasure and satisfaction that you derive
from using it ; the immense saving in time, energy,
temper, boots and clothing, to say nothing of ammunition,
for which it is directly responsible by enabling you to kill
clean instead of only wounding and having to follow up

an animal; besides those occasions when you are
shooting for an absolutely empty pot—the wind contrary,
blowing from each and every point of the compass in
turn, and the game very much on the alert—when you
are enabled to drop a beast from a range from which you
would never dream of attempting a shot with any ordinary
sights. I surely do not begrudge one penny of the amount
I spent on my 'scope sights.

One can readily appreciate why men consider a 'scope
sight slow if they have only used a 'scope mounted away
up high over the barrel, because they have nothing
against which to rest their cheek and steady their head ;
the result is that the head moves about and therefore the
man cannot bring the animal into focus. A rifle is fitted
with a butt so that you can rest your cheek against it when
aiming ; a telescope sight is added to still further assist
you to take an accurate aim (there is *no* other object in
having a 'scope sight—it is *not* fitted merely for the
benefit of the lazy man who cannot be bothered trying to
get any closer to the game) ; yet men who have their
'scope sights mounted away up in the air, calmly, deliberately, and of their own free will, throw away that
first and most important aid to steady aiming ! If a 'scope
sight is mounted flat down over the action or barrels of
the rifle, so that it can be used as easily, comfortably and
efficiently as can the open sights, it will be found that
it is even quicker than the open sights. There is nothing
slow about a low-powered sight so mounted.

Then, to take the final charge in the indictment—that
it is a liability when facing a charging lion. If you have
opened fire on, say, a lion and lioness having a feed at
the edge of the reeds or bush, and have deemed it advisable to use your 'scope sight so as to ensure clean kills
and avoid having to follow a wounded beast into that
cover ; you have killed the lion, and now find yourself
being charged by the lioness as so often happens in a case
of this description. Well, my own opinion is that you

will stop that lioness with a much greater degree of certainty with a low-mounted 'scope sight than you will with any other kind of sight because of the perfect view you have and the ease of aiming without having to rapidly alter the focus of your eye from backsight to foresight and to the lioness to make sure that you have your sights in line. You will experience a curious impersonal sensation which will prevent you becoming flurried—how can I put it ?—it is as though you are seated in a cinema and watching a picture taken by a man who knew his job : a lion is charging the camera (though, of course, you cannot see the camera) and it looks as though that lion was just going to leap right out through the screen and land in your lap ; there is a thrill attached to it, but it is a curious impersonal kind of thrill, because you know that you are actually in no sort of danger whatsoever : you are not frightened and you are not flurried, and if the attendant had allowed you to bring a rifle into the theatre with you, you could easily put a bullet into the centre of that lion's chest. That, as nearly as I can describe it, is precisely what I felt when charged by lion on each occasion when I was armed with a 'scope-sighted rifle. I prefer a low-mounted telescope sight to any other kind of sight for use on such occasions.

There are a number of problems connected with the mounting of a telescope sight into which we need not enter here. Suffice it to say, that if you want satisfaction from your telescope sight you must pay for it. As with a camera, the whole secret is in the lens : the better the lens, the better the results. No cheaply-mounted tele-scope sight can possibly retain accuracy after many rounds have been fired. It will inevitably become loose under the constant shock of discharge, and consequently its position will certainly vary slightly in between shots, and since the whole idea of a telescope sight is to give greater precision in shooting, it is absolutely imperative that it should be so mounted that it will retain its rigidity.

For instance, many of the cheap Continental rifles in general use—particularly Mannlicher-Schonauers—can be bought with an inexpensive telescope sight for a few pounds extra. It is little more than money wasted. Sooner or later you will be disappointed. And this does not only apply to cheap Continental mountings ; it applies equally to cheap British or cheap American mountings. Personally, I have only used 'scope sights mounted by Holland, Rigby and Jeffery on big game rifles, and by Parker-Hale on miniature rifles, and needless to say have found them all to be most excellent. I have discussed telescope sights with a number of men and I must say that those who were disappointed and disgusted outnumbered by no small degree those who were thoroughly satisfied ; but then it is only fair and truthful to add that those who had been using cheap sights cheaply mounted were in a considerable majority.

Another very great advantage of telescope sights is that they enable men whose sight is failing to continue hunting when, with ordinary sights, they would be compelled to give it up. As an illustration of which I might mention that I know, personally, a very keen German hunter with a quite considerable experience of elephant whose sight has been failing for some time and who is so short-sighted now that even in close scrub country he invariably carries a pair of x6 Zeiss binoculars round his neck. His battery consists of two best-quality British-built doubles—a Holland ·465 " Royal " and an Evans ·450—both fitted with the most enormous bead foresights that I have ever seen—he could not see anything smaller—and a 'scope-sighted Mauser which he describes as a 9·5 mm. " Special " and which is really just a German version of our ·375 magnum (it is probably the new 9·3 × 64 mm. Brenneke). His trackers point in the required direction when they spot the game, " M " uses his binoculars to see whatever there may be to be seen, and then takes over his 'scope-sighted magazine rifle. Although he is compelled to use his doubles when tackling elephant at very close quarters in thick cover, he kills more of them with his 'scope-sighted magazine rifle than with any other weapon. Were there no such things as telescope sights, he would be incapable of carrying on.

TRAJECTORIES

As I have already stated, the trajectory tables which I have given at the end of this chapter are taken with the author's kind and generous permission from *Notes on Sporting Rifles*. It will be noticed that the rifles are all sighted so that they will group approximately centrally in a 4-inch bull at 100 yards ; and that is really all that you need to bother about when ordering a rifle : just insist on your gunsmith taking the " six o'clock " aim at a 4-inch bull at 100 yards and making the rifle group not lower than centrally in the bull—then test it yourself and make sure that he has done so. With the exception of the ·577 and ·600 bores, which should be made to group along the bottom edge of the bull (or, perhaps better, centrally in the bull at 50 yards), have all your rifles sighted in this manner and you will not have to bother about estimating ranges or altering elevations.

In connection with these trajectories, the following are Major Burrard's own words :

The trajectories given are those obtained with ordinary sporting rifles fitted with 24-inch barrels in the case of those weapons which are usually made in magazine form, and 26-inch barrels in the case of doubles. In actual practice the charge of powder used in a double is slightly less than that used in a similar magazine-actioned rifle so as to allow a slightly larger margin for excess pressure. The result of this is that the M.V. from a double is not quite so great as that given by a single rifle, and the resulting trajectories will be found to be approximately the same if the double is fitted with slightly longer barrels.

Allowance has been made in every case for the actual line of sight being above the centre of the bore. . . .

The plus sign denotes the rise of the bullet above and the minus sign the drop of the bullet below the line of sight at the particular ranges given.

For purposes of practical convenience the intermediate distances for rifles which should be sighted for 150 and 175 yards have in both cases been given as 100 yards. This will enable the sighting of all rifles to be carried out at this convenient range. As a matter of fact, the culminating points of the trajectories actually occur approximately at 80 and 90 yards respectively, but the figures given for 100 yards may be taken as being sufficiently near, for all practical purposes, to the actual greatest rise of the bullet above the line of sight in each case.

It should be born in mind that if a rifle is sighted for 150 yards, or any other distance for that matter, its trajectory is not merely flat for the bare 150 yards for which it is sighted, but for some distance beyond that point. The distance will, of course, vary with each different calibre depending on the bullet's capacity for overcoming the air-resistance, but the trajectory will be flat, for all practical purposes of sport, until the bullet has dropped, say, 3 inches below the line of sight. So that, speaking generally, if your rifle is sighted for 150 yards you can consider that it has a flat trajectory for at least 175 yards, possibly more ; and the same applies to all other ranges for which rifles may be sighted : the weapon will have a flat trajectory for at least a further 25 or 30 yards.

RIFLES WHICH SHOULD BE SIGHTED FOR 100 YARDS

Rifle.	Bullet.	Ranges in yards.					
		50	100	150	200	250	300
·577 . .	750	+2·1	o	− 3·8	− 11·4	—	—
·375 . .	270	+2·1	o	− 3·7	− 10·7	− 21·4	− 36·3
·400/·360 .	300	+2·25	o	− 3·9	− 11·2	− 22·4	− 37·8

RIFLES WHICH WILL STAND SIGHTING FOR 150 YARDS

Rifle.	Bullet.	Ranges in yards.				
		100	150	200	250	300
·505	525	+2·0	0	− 4·9	− 13·0	− 25·4
·500	570	+2·2	0	− 5·2	− 14·0	− 27·0
·476	520	+2·2	0	− 5·2	− 13·5	− 26·0
·475	480	+2·2	0	− 5·1	− 13·1	− 25·3
·475 No. 2 . . .	480	+2·2	0	− 5·0	− 13·0	− 24·6
·470	500	+2·2	0	− 5·0	− 13·0	− 24·5
·465	480	+2·2	0	− 5·0	− 13·0	− 24·5
·425	410	+1·7	0	− 4·2	− 10·8	− 20·6
·423 (10·75 mm.) .	347	+2·2	0	− 5·1	− 13·2	− 25·5
·416	410	+1·7	0	− 4·0	− 10·5	− 19·7
·405 Winchester .	300	+2·2	0	− 5·3	− 14·0	− 27·0
·400 Jeffery . . .	400	+2·1	0	− 4·9	− 12·6	− 23·9
·366 (9·3 mm.) . .	285	+2·0	0	− 5·0	− 12·0	− 22·5
·360 No. 2 . . .	320	+2·1	0	− 4·4	− 11·8	− 21·8
·400/·350 . . .	310	+2·1	0	− 4·9	− 12·6	− 24·0
·350 Winchester .	200	+2·4	0	− 5·4	− 15·3	− 29·2
·318	250	+1·7	0	− 4·0	− 10·4	− 19·6
·303 Mark VI . .	215	+2·3	0	− 5·4	− 14·2	− 27·0
·275 (7 mm.) . .	173	+1·9	0	− 4·5	− 11·2	− 21·3

RIFLES WHICH WILL STAND SIGHTING FOR 175 YARDS

Rifle.	Bullet.	Ranges in yards.				
		100	175	200	250	300
·404	300	+2·3	0	− 1·8	− 7·1	− 15·0
·375 Magnum . .	270	+2·0	0	− 1·5	− 6·0	− 13·0
·375 ,, . .	300	+2·4	0	− 1·9	− 7·4	− 15·4
·350 ,, . .	225	+2·2	0	− 1·7	− 6·9	− 14·4
·333	250	+2·3	0	− 1·7	− 6·9	− 14·7
·318	180	+2·0	0	− 1·6	− 6·4	− 13·6
·303 Mark VII . .	176	+2·4	0	− 1·7	− 7·4	− 15·7
·300 Springfield . .	150	+2·0	0	− 1·6	− 6·2	− 13·2
·300 ,, . .	180	+2·3	0	− 1·75	− 7·0	− 14·8
·256 (old 6·5 mm.) .	156	+2·5	0	− 2·1	− 8·0	− 16·6

RIFLES WHICH WILL STAND SIGHTING FOR 200 YARDS

Rifle.	Bullet.	Ranges in yards.			
		100	200	250	300
·375 Magnum . . .	235	+ 2·4	o	− 4·0	− 10·5
·330	165	+ 2·2	o	− 3·5	− 9·2
·375/·300	150	+ 2·0	o	− 3·0	− 8·0
·375/·300	180	+ 2·4	o	− 4·0	− 9·7
·280	140	+ 2·0	o	− 3·0	− 8·0
·280	160	+ 2·2	o	− 4·0	− 9·7
·275 Magnum . . .	160	+ 2·2	o	− 4·0	− 9·7
·275 Rigby	140	+ 2·5	o	− 3·7	− 9·25
·260	110	+ 1·9	o	− 2·9	− 7·5
·256 Magnum . . .	135	+ 2·5	o	− 4·5	− 10·0
·250 Savage	87	+ 2·2	o	− 3·5	− 9·2
·240	100	+ 2·0	o	− 3·0	− 7·8

CHAPTER XIII

Miscellaneous Odds and Ends and After-Thoughts

CLEANING RIFLES

ONE frequently hears men grumble that they can only fire a matter of a few hundred rounds through their rifles before the barrels are worn out. Of two men whom I knew, each armed with a Westley Richards ·425-bore magazine rifle, one grumbled that he had only fired 200 rounds whilst the other complained that his barrel had been worn out by the time that he had fired a bare 120 rounds through it !

Now this is absurd. No rifle worthy of the name could possibly be " worn out " after so very few rounds had been fired through it. It was corrosion, and rust, which ate away their barrels through their ignorance of the correct method of cleaning nitro-firing rifles, together with their carelessness and laziness over the necessity for promptly cleaning the weapons on getting back to camp. The usual method they adopt is to throw themselves down in an easy chair and tell their gunbearer to clean the rifle ; the lad, knowing no better, pulls a dirty rag through it two or three times and brings it along for his master to examine. Having recently been fired and then pulled through, it looks reasonably bright and not too clogged up, so he tells the boy he had better put some oil in it. The lad goes along, collects that same dirty old rag, dips it in some old motor oil in the sump of the lorry or even in a puddle of oil that may have dripped out on the ground from the back axle, and pulls that through the barrel and then wipes over the outside of the weapon with his oily hands and puts it away in the tent or hut, where it remains unlooked at until next required for use. When it is wanted, the owner has a look through it and, needless to say, finds it all bunged up with rust and muck. He tells the boy to clean it, and the lad does the best he can with that same treasured old rag, but naturally cannot make much impression. The white man, impatient to be off, takes it from him and loads up with the remark that, " it doesn't matter—the first shot will clear all that muck out of it ! . . ."

As soon as you return to camp your first thought should be for your rifle. The following method of cleaning I have always found most effective : Pour boiling water through the bore until the barrel is thoroughly heated, then dry this out. Now dip a phosphor-bronze brush (brass brushes last no time and the bristles are liable to drop into the extractor mechanism as they break off ; hard steel brushes are apt to scratch the bore—I have never used mild steel brushes, so cannot say how they behave ; but the bronze ones are excellent) in Young's ·303 combined cleaner and rust preventer, B.S.A. " Kleenwell " oil, or other good rifle oil, and thoroughly scour out the bore. These alkaline oils will neutralize any acid fouling, whilst the wire brush will loosen all the fouling and get rid of any metallic fouling that may be there (the boiling water has already dissolved the cap residue). Now dip a stiff bristle brush in any one of these good oils and wash out all the fouling loosened by the wire brush, some of which may have remained. Then use clean flannel strips (patches) on the jag of the cleaning rod and rub these through the bore again and again until a clean patch rubbed through the bore comes out as clean as it went in : if it does not come out clean then the bore cannot be clean, or what marked the patch ? If you do not stint the oil, but are generous with it on the bristle brush, the patches have little to do but wipe out this surplus oil ; you will probably find that a couple of them are ample. But if you stint the oil, or cannot be bothered to use the bristle brush after the wire brush, you will be giving yourself needless

11

labour trying to clean the bore with dry patches—the oil does the actual cleaning : the patches are really only required to wipe out the surplus oil.

Now dip a wool mop in Young's ·303 oil and rub it through the bore so as to leave a film of oil which will dry on and prevent rust. I know of nothing better, or even so good, as Young's oil for this purpose ; you can put your rifle away for months if necessary and not worry about it : when you come to use it again and wipe it out, you will find it bright and shining. If you are using " Kleenwell " oil, and there is certainly nothing better for washing out the bore, it can safely be left in the barrel as a rust preventer but not for long periods, because it is primarily intended for washing out the bore and is consequently made very thin. This means that if the barrel is hot, as it probably is after the boiling water, the " Kleenwell " oil will tend to run down to the lowest part of the bore when the rifle is put away, leaving but a very, very thin film behind it. If you have no Young's oil, therefore, you should use B.S.A. " Safetipaste " : this is a strongly alkaline thick grease which will absolutely prevent rusting for any length of time ; but it is not quite so easy to ensure a perfect film of grease throughout the bore as it is to ensure a film of oil. Rust cannot form in the presence of an alkali.

Naturally, any oil or grease must be completely removed from the bore before the rifle is fired ; otherwise excessive pressures may be set up, and in the case of a generous quantity of thick grease the barrel might even be bulged, though I do not think that there would be any likelihood or danger of it bursting. The easiest way to thoroughly remove oil or grease is to dip a clean rag in petrol or paraffin (petrol is the better because any left in the bore will evaporate) and run this through the bore two or three times, then wipe out with a clean cloth. As far as oil in the bore is concerned, particularly in a hot climate, it is improbable that you would seriously injure your rifle if you were to fire it without first wiping out the oil ; but the oil will certainly interfere with the grouping of the shots—the rifle will not shoot as accurately as it normally would.

If you clean your rifles in the manner which I have detailed above, you will not be counting the number of rounds which you fire through it in mere hundreds, but in thousands—quite literally. Any good barrel that has been properly looked after should be capable of firing anything from 4,000 to 5,000 rounds, or even more, at sporting ranges before it will require replacing with a new one. In other words, there should never be any question of a barrel being " worn out "—at least not where a non-professional hunter is concerned.

For the locks and action mechanism of your double rifles, you should use a special lock oil which you can get from your gunsmith ; but if you happen to run out of it, " 3-in-1 " oil, which is obtainable anywhere, is an excellent substitute : I have used it from the Arctic to the Equator and found it will not dry, gum, or clog in any climate.

If there are man-eating lions about, or if for any other reason you think that you may be wanting a rifle during the night, or if you think that you may want it at any moment during the day and in either event have wiped the oil out of it, you should certainly have a muzzle cover to slip on. It is amazing the things that can and do get down the bore : during the day I have known large hornets of the type that build those mud nests in your rooms, build two of these nests several inches down the bores of a large-bore double rifle so that they were quite invisible unless the breech was broken and one looked down the barrels—had that rifle been fired without examination, in all probability a new pair of barrels would have been required if nothing worse. In the same way, you should always carry a pull-through with you when out hunting since it is very easy for things to drop down the muzzles when the rifle is stood against a tree ; which, of course implies that you should make a point of looking through the barrels after standing your rifle against anything in that manner.

And here I should like to stress the importance of testing the working of every part of the mechanism of whatever weapons you are taking out with you that day *before leaving camp.* I had this most forcibly impressed upon me not very long ago when I was charged by a buffalo of whose very existence I was totally unaware and which, as I afterwards discovered, had been wounded a day or so before by some native armed with an old gas-pipe muzzle-loader. The particular rifle which I intended using that day had had a few days rest, and although I thought that I had cleaned and oiled it thoroughly before putting it away, I had apparently forgotten that it had been an exceptionally hot day the last time it was used and the sweat from my hand had managed to find its way under the safety slide (and there are few things that cause rust to form more quickly than human perspiration does) and the result of this was, that when I tried to manipulate the slide I found that a terrific effort was necessary ; accordingly, I unloaded and with a tooth-brush dipped in oil did the necessary and put things right. Had it not been for the habit of mine of testing things before leaving camp, that buffalo would almost certainly have got me. The killers do not loiter when on the warpath and in any case do not speak your language, so it is of no earthly use trying to explain to one of them that your rifle has jammed and that it is not your fault !

SAFETIES

Unless otherwise ordered, the safety slide on double rifles is almost invariably made automatic as on a shot-gun. That is, that the act of opening the breech—or rather, of moving the lever across to permit of the breech being opened—puts the safety slide back in the " safe " position.

Now, where rifles which are solely intended—or at any rate, primarily intended—for use against dangerous game at close quarters are concerned, this, to my way of thinking, is little short of criminal thoughtlessness on the part of gunsmiths. Any experienced hunter knows the danger of automatic safeties and can order his doubles to be built with non-automatic safeties ; but an inexperienced man would in all probability never think of such an apparently very small point.

Most gunsmiths pass over the question in the catalogues with a small footnote to the effect that, " These rifles can be had with automatic or non-automatic safeties ", or words to that effect. Jeffery is better than most, for he definitely recommends non-automatic safeties if the rifle is intended for use against dangerous game, in two different places in his catalogue ; and he gives his reasons for recommending the non-automatic.

But that is not sufficient. In my opinion, *all* double rifles—other, perhaps, than ultra-small bores—should be built with non-automatic safeties unless the purchaser definitely orders an automatic safety. After all, no magazine rifle for obvious reasons has ever been built with an automatic safety, yet how many accidents are there through men forgetting to put the safety catch " on " after firing ? And even if there were occasional accidents through doubles being fitted with non-automatic safeties and the owners forgetting to draw back the slide when they have finished firing, I should be prepared to wager a considerable sum that they would be far less frequent than the " accidents " which can and do arise through men forgetting, in the excitement of the moment, to push an automatic safety forward again after reloading when they want to fire another quick shot in an emergency. Why should they be any more liable to forget to put the safety " on " after they have finished using a double than they would with a magazine ?

It is extremely improbable that there is a single, solitary man in the length and breadth of Africa who learnt to shoot with a double rifle ; but, on the contrary, practically every man has used magazine rifles for years prior to using his first double. And since with magazine rifles, having turned the safety over into the firing position immediately prior to the shot he can then forget all about it until the shooting is over, he naturally, subconsciously, comes to feel that having put the safety in the firing position on a double he has not got to think of it again until he has finished with the rifle.

And this is what gives rise to so many uncomfortably close shaves, if nothing worse, in the Bush. I have had no unpleasant experiences of this description myself, because prior to using my first double I had heard a man telling of a narrow escape which he had had through using an automatic safety—though he did not appear to realize that it was the rifle that was to blame ; he merely stated that having reloaded, he completely forgot to push forward the slide again ; but although it was some years afterwards before I got my first hammerless double, I never forgot and insisted on a non-automatic safety. But in lieu of an experience of my own, that related by Commander Blunt on the occasion when he was tackling that large herd of elephant to which I have already, in a previous chapter, referred, will bear repetition here.

Blunt, having shot several of the herd, found himself surrounded by elephant that he could not see in the bush and grass. He came on a solitary bull and killed him.

. . . next second [he writes], a panic-stricken party of cows and calves came crashing through the bush on my left about 6 abreast and 4 deep. There was no evading them, so I threw up my rifle, but *found the safety catch on.* I had just time to blaze off a round, dropping one cow, but this did not stop them, so I fired my last cartridge and dropped another cow. This effectually checked the stampede, and they stood for some moments undecided which way to go. . . . My gunbearer and I "froze", the distance between us and the leading elephant being only 8 paces. [The italics are mine.]

Now Commander Blunt omits to tell us what rifle he was using on this occasion ; though in a later chapter he states : "the Rigby ·416 magazine I have always used ". But there can be no possible doubt that he was not using his ·416 on this day. Because all powerful magazine rifles—the ·416 included—are fitted with a Mauser pattern bolt action on which the safety must be turned across from one side to the other—an operation which requires a certain degree of effort : it could not possibly be turned over accidentally. And if Commander Blunt is to be taken literally—and there is no earthly reason why he should not be taken literally— then, since "next second" the cows and calves came stampeding towards him, it is inconceivable that he could have recharged his magazine, closed the bolt and turned over the safety—and then forgotten that he had done so. Besides which, it is equally inconceivable that he would have put the safety "on" before making sure that the bull was dead and not merely stunned, since he had, presumably, dropped him with a side brain shot—particularly when he knew that he was surrounded by upwards of 80 elephant.

From all of which it will, I think, be perfectly obvious that Commander Blunt could not have been using his beloved ·416—nor any other magazine rifle for that matter—on this particular occasion. But give him a double—a double which had, very unwisely, been fitted with an automatic safety—and the entire episode is perfectly explained : He dropped the bull, lowered the rifle, broke the breech—which act put the safety "on"— and was probably just slipping another cartridge into the right barrel before closing in to make sure that the bull was dead, when the cows and calves broke through the bush beside him. He snaps-to the breech, throws the

rifle to his shoulder—and finds the safety " on " . . .
Now had he and his gunbearer been standing just a trifle
closer to that bush they might very easily, and in all
probability would, have been killed. And all because
some idiot of a gunsmith had sold him a double rifle
fitted with an automatic safety !

Again. A hunter was killed by a lion in Northern
Rhodesia quite recently. He was using a double. His
boys, who were eyewitnesses of the incident, tell us that
" H " fired at and wounded a lion which promptly
charged. The hunter was seen to lower the rifle from
his shoulder for a moment or two, and then raise it
again and wait—but he never fired the shot for which
they were all waiting. Now, beyond the fact that it was
a double, I know nothing whatever about the rifle that
he was using ; but I venture to suggest that in all probability an automatic safety was responsible for his death.
Let us picture what might, and in all probability actually
did, happen : " H ", seeing the lion charge on receipt
of the first bullet, lowered the butt of the rifle from his
shoulder and broke the breech with the intention of
reloading, thus putting the safety " on ". Then, realiz-
ing that he would not have time in which to complete
the operation, snapped-to the breech and raised the rifle,
waiting until the lion was practically on him so as to
make absolutely certain of the shot since he had but
the one, only to realize when it was too late that he
had forgotten to push forward the safety again after breaking the breech that time. . . . Could anything be more
inherently probable ? Possibly, had he succeeded in reloading, he might have remembered to push forward
the safety again ; but not having actually reloaded he
forgot all about it—never gave it a thought until too
late.

I have gone into this question of safeties in some
detail and at considerable length, because I consider that
it is a matter of the utmost importance. I have heard

a number of men relate unpleasant experiences entirely due to this cause.

Non-automatic safeties are the only kind that should ever be fitted to double rifles if there is the slightest possibility of the weapons being taken against dangerous game.

Auctor : Yes, I fully agree with all that. But tell me, what happens if one finds that the excellent second-hand rifle that one wants to buy is fitted with an automatic safety ? Can it be converted to non-automatic ? And if so, will it be a frightfully expensive business ?

Lector : No decent gunsmith from whom you are buying a second-hand double rifle would charge you a sixpence for converting an automatic safety to non-automatic. It is only necessary to remove the little connecting rod between the top lever and the safety slide —a matter of only a few minutes with a side lock action ; a little longer with a box lock. If you already have a double fitted with an automatic safety, the gunsmith from whom you bought it will probably convert it for nothing —if he does charge you anything, it will only be a matter of a very few shillings. Decide for yourself whether or not your life is worth that amount.

CARRYING RIFLES

The great majority of men in Africa never think of taking over their rifles until they sight the game. This, in my opinion, is a great mistake. In thick cover or broken scrub country the game may sight you at least as soon as you sight them. If you have to take over your rifle from your gunbearer, by the time you have done so and prepared it for action, the game may have stampeded.

Save in absolutely open country where the game can invariably be seen from afar, the sportsman when actually hunting should always carry whichever of his weapons he is most likely to require. And since it is far easier and—as I shall presently show—far better to carry the rifle by the sling, a good sling is essential. It should not be attached with spring hook swivels—they rattle and clink and generally make a noise ; if the rifle has eyes the sling should have tapered ends—these can be threaded through the eyes and fastened with a couple of half-hitches. Personally, however, I much prefer broad sling swivels on the rifle, and always order them on a new weapon ; in the method of carrying a rifle which I am going to suggest they are better than eyes because they absolutely ensure that the sling slides down off your shoulder, whereas with eyes it *might* not do so with quite the same degree of certainty.

Of course, when after elephant it is not always necessary to take over your rifle until you sight or hear the herd other, perhaps, than in long grass. Nevertheless, you will by no means infrequently encounter a lone bull un- expectedly when following up a herd, and if you are not carrying a rifle yourself you may lose a good chance if he happens to wind you.

I have vivid recollections of just such an occasion some years ago in the Moravia district in the Lower Zambezi Valley. I had been following up a small mixed herd since daybreak, but the wind was contrary, blowing from all points of the compass in succession, and they would not let me catch up with them. I had halted for 20 minutes at midday by a small stream, and we all had a feed. Then we continued along the spoor in the swelter- ing heat of those hottest hours of the day, 12 to 3, in the hope that the breeze which had died down would stay like that. For I knew that the elephant would be wanting to halt also. As it was comparatively open country amongst low hills with just a few scattered trees here and there, offering practically nothing in the way of shade, I gave my tracker—who is also my head gun- bearer—my heavy double to carry in front of me, and my second gunbearer my lighter weapon to carry immedi- ately behind me. Needless to say, there was not an elephant in sight, nor did we expect to see any until we had reached somewhat closer bush.

The heat of the sun and the infinitely worse heat which was flung up in our faces from the scorching ground—it was like the blast from an open furnace door—on top of the meal which we had just consumed, added to the utter improbability of encountering elephant, made us all a trifle drowsy and careless. I gradually dropped behind my tracker—an unprecedented thing for me to do—whilst my second gunbearer, in the same way, lolled along farther and farther behind me. And then, quite suddenly, I looked up and saw a splendid tusker coming towards us diagonally across the open and *not 50 paces away*! We, as it were, were cutting across his bows; and it looked as though he and my tracker were just going to meet in about two minutes! I was a good 40 paces behind the lad so looked round to grab my second rifle from the boy who should have been immediately behind me; but he was as far from me as I was from my tracker. And there I stood making frantic signs and signals in a vain endeavour to attract his attention and have him run up with the rifle. But it was no use—he was walking in an even deeper sleep than that in which I had been! And it was as I turned to shout to my tracker to draw his attention to the fact that he and the elephant were on the point of meeting—there was nothing else that I could do—that he at last woke up himself. On seeing the elephant—by this time not 10 yards away from him—he jumped about 3 feet in the air and legged it back to me with the rifle. And curiously enough, it was only then that the elephant saw *him*. The big fellow must have caught an eddy of wind from us to him when he was on the farther side of a small hill—*kopje*, they would call it, south of the Zambezi—and was running as he thought from danger. For he had been walking just as fast as he could without actually running—that deceptively fast, shambling gait of a badly frightened elephant. All his faculties must have been concentrated on his rear, where he thought that the danger was—which explains why he also was so unobservant. He slewed round and broke into a run, and it was almost sun-down before I caught up with him again and succeeded in bagging him. Had I been carrying a rifle myself, I could have dropped him then and there, and saved myself all that additional fatigue.

On another occasion, only a few days ago, I was out looking for some meat for my lads. Hunting dogs, however, had been through the district during the night and although I had been out since daybreak and it was now close on midday, I had not seen a living thing. The heat was appalling—this district round my old camp at Mangwendi is the hottest in which I have ever hunted —and I had just handed my rifle over to my tracker and was suggesting a return to camp, when I spotted what looked for all the world like 4 or 5 lions lying amongst some small boulders between a few stunted trees. The grass had long been burnt off, and there was not a scrap of cover in between us ; so I just started walking slowly towards them as though to pass slightly to one side. The closer that we got, the more certain did we become that they were indeed lions ; so I again took over my rifle. But, on closing in to about 40 or 50 paces, we were compelled to admit that they were only boulders after all. I handed the rifle back to Saduko and laughed with him at the idea of our stalking a few stones in spite of all our experience ! We had just turned to continue the tramp back to camp when I found myself looking straight at a splendid Sable bull at not more than 30 to 40 paces at the most ! He was standing right out in the open watching us—head up and ears cocked—motionless. He had not stampeded sooner because all animals know that there is not much immediate danger about noisy creatures —men who wander about talking and laughing are not hunting, any more than are lions when they go roaring

around. Both Saduko and myself had had our every
sense concentrated on what we thought were lions and
consequently never dreamt of seeing any other game so
close—particularly after such a fruitless morning.

All of this to show how you can meet game at close
quarters in the most unlikely places and under the most
unexpected circumstances and, therefore, how necessary
it is that you should always carry a rifle yourself. Even
if your gunbearer is close to you, it is almost inevitable
that you will make a hasty grab for the rifle in order to
get a shot. Any sudden movement of that description
will stampede the game ; whereas, if you are carrying
the rifle yourself you can swing it into action without
making any sudden or jerky movements.

In thick cover you should always carry the double yourself—particularly does this apply when hunting or even
walking through dense bush in which rhino may be
encountered and therefore wherein you may be attacked
without the slightest warning or provocation from very
close quarters. I have already described how I have
had one very unpleasant encounter, and I have been
attacked on several other occasions in a very similar
manner though not quite so successfully from the rhino's
point of view !

In thick cover, that is, wherein you may want the rifle
with the least possible delay, I have always found the
following by far the best method of carrying the rifle :
Carry the rifle with the sling over your right shoulder
(assuming that you shoot from the right shoulder) and
the rifle upsidedown, muzzles foremost. The muzzles
are kept pointing up at an angle of about 45° and steadied
by the right hand on the barrels and the right forearm
and elbow pressing against it (the sling should be shortened to permit of this being done). If you want the rifle
quickly it is only necessary to drop your right hand to
the grip and turn the barrels uppermost, at the same time
as the left hand comes across and grasps the barrels. The

sling will slide off your shoulder and slip down past your
elbow as you turn the barrels uppermost ; but to make
quite certain that there will be no hitch, it is advisable
to have flat sling swivels on your rifles : eyes are not
quite so certain. The rifle is pointing in the direction
in which it is most likely to be required, and has been
got ready for action with the least possible delay and—
a very important point—with the least possible amount
of movement on your part. If you carry it as so many
men do who carry their own rifles, more or less vertically
behind the shoulder with the sling to the front, then
before it can be brought into action it must be swung
round past your elbow. This, besides taking longer,
means considerably more movement on your part ; whilst
there is always the possibility of the rifle either knocking
loudly against a tree or something or brushing against
twigs or leaves—it might even get hung up on a trailing
vine.

If you are carrying the rifle on your shoulder without
a sling, in the first place you will probably find it more
tiring, and in the second place it also stands a very good
chance of the muzzles knocking against something on
your bringing it down. If you are not carrying your rifle
yourself, but have left it to your gunbearer, then in my
opinion there is only one way in which he should be
trained to carry it, and that is : a pace and a half in front
of you—just far enough in front, that is, to prevent you
treading on his heels and yet at the same time sufficiently
close to enable you to just reach out a hand if necessary
and grab it off his shoulder. And what is more, he must
carry it on his shoulder and *muzzles foremost.*

Now many men condemn this method as they say that
it " strains " the rifle. How *can* it " strain " the rifle ?
The boy will carry the rifle in the easiest possible manner
—that is, with the point of balance just over his shoulder,
or rather, just behind it, so that the muzzles (or butt, as
the case may be) will press up slightly against his hand.

Obviously, therefore, no matter whether the rifle is butt-foremost or muzzle-foremost, the amount of " strain " must be exactly the same in either event. The object in carrying the rifle muzzle-foremost is that it is always pointing in the direction in which it is most likely to be required—a very great advantage in very thick cover wherein the muzzles or foresight block can very easily become entangled in things if the rifle has to be twisted or turned round. Besides which, the rifle can be brought to bear far more rapidly. I was mighty glad that I had trained my gunbearer to carry my rifle in that manner on the occasion when that rhino tossed me over his head !

When hunting in more open country, it is quite permissible to carry the rifle with the sling to the front and the rifle vertically behind the shoulder, and it will probably be found to be the easiest way. For the first few days you may find the rifle becoming rather a load after a few hours, but you will soon become accustomed to it and will not notice the weight.

I have often heard men say that they would never use a rifle with a sling on it in thick cover owing to the possibilities of the sling becoming entangled in things. Well that may be so if the sling is very long ; but if you carry the rifle in the manner which I suggest, you will want a fairly short sling ; and in twenty-five years of hunting I have never yet had a sling become entangled in anything.

Another small point in connection with carrying rifles : Many men who possess good weapons carry them in covers, even when actually hunting, if there is the slightest possibility of rain. This I consider is very unwise because you can easily loose a good chance owing to the length of time that is required to undo the buckles of the cover and draw out your rifle. (I have even known men who would not go out in the rain, although game was reported close by, for fear of getting their rifles wet !) Your rifle is not made of sugar ; it will not melt. If there is any fear of it doing so, then you would be well advised to discard it and get a better one. Provided that you clean your rifles thoroughly and use a good alkaline oil and plenty of it, it matters not how wet they get when hunting. One of the most successful elephant hunts that it has ever been my good fortune to enjoy took place during one of the worst thunderstorms that I have ever experienced.

It was up amongst the hills on the Angoni plateau in Portuguese East. I had been following a troop of five large bulls for some hours, and eventually caught up with them on the side of a hill amongst rocks and scattered trees—five splendid tuskers. I was shooting on licence, and had just taken out a new permit which gave me the right to kill five bulls. A black thunderstorm which I had been watching for some time broke directly overhead at the very instant that I fired for the leader of the troop : a blinding flash, which stood quivering and trembling close beside us for an appreciable time, followed, instantaneously, by an ear-splitting detonation. The crashing roar of my big Express—I was using a Jeffery double ·600 Nitro—was completely drowned ; the master bull dropped with a side brain shot ; and I reloaded that barrel. Again I fired, and again the report of the rifle was swamped in the vastly greater report of the heavier artillery ; and another bull went down. The three wretched elephant which remained were panic-stricken with the thunder and lightning and with seeing two of their leaders collapse. They milled round in a small circle unable to make up their minds which way to run. I killed them all ; and I honestly do not think that any one of them knew that a rifle had been fired, although only one of the following three shots synchronized with a crash of thunder. There was a regular cloud-burst along with the rest and the water was actually over my ankles although it was running down the side of the hill in a great sheet. But my rifle never suffered ;

yet some idea of the violence of the rain may be gathered from the fact that I had to have my lad hold both his hat and mine over the barrels owing to the extent to which the rain was bouncing and dancing on the barrels and rib, completely preventing me from seeing even the backsight.

SECOND-HAND RIFLES

If you feel that you really cannot rise to a new " Best " double rifle—and they are an expensive proposition for a poor man—and you are contemplating a second-hand one, then the best and most satisfactory procedure is to get it from the makers. They all have used rifles of their own make—probably taken in exchange for new weapons, or handed back by wealthy sportsmen to sell for them —always on sale, and such weapons are guaranteed to be in sound, serviceable condition. It would no more pay a good firm to sell you a second-hand " dud " than it would to sell you a new " dud " : competition is much too keen nowadays, and no firm can live on a reputation gained fifty or one hundred years ago : every weapon of their own make that they sell must live up to that reputation or they will soon have to close their doors. You need not have the slightest qualms. If by any chance you have decided upon a weapon which was not built by the firm from which you are buying it, if you take the number and have it verified by the maker you will be quite safe. Unfortunately, it is not unknown for unscrupulous firms to engrave the name of one of the best makers on an inferior weapon ; but if you verify the number you will be all right. A further incentive to deal only with sound, reputable firms.

The choice of any particular firm of gunsmiths is rather like the choice of anything else : cars, motor-cycles and so on. Some are definitely better than others ; they build better-balanced and more highly-finished weapons usually —though not by any means always—at a higher price.

But price is not necessarily a criterion.   Some firms have vastly greater expenses than others : high rentals, over-head expenses, elaborate showrooms and all the rest of it, and consequently must fix their prices with a view to recovering these expenses as well as to leave a fair and reasonable margin over for legitimate profits.   Personally, I have always preferred Holland & Holland for doubles and John Rigby for magazines ; but I should not like to think that that remark would be taken as disparaging to Holland's magazines or to Rigby's doubles.   On the con-trary, nobody could build better doubles than John Rigby builds—the matter is solely and entirely a question of personal preference.   I do not think that any man with any pretensions to being in his right mind could possibly criticize adversely weapons of any type built by either firm.

I have and always have had a very great weakness for Jeffery's best-quality rifles—both double and magazine. I have had no personal experience of his second-quality rifles, so cannot discuss them ; I will just say this : that were I to find myself with one in my hands now, I should use it with every confidence.   But I can speak from personal experience of his best-quality weapons—and I can honestly and truthfully state that I have never handled more accurate, more reliable, or more perfectly balanced rifles than Jeffery's best-quality doubles.   The first Jeffery rifle that I ever used was a double ·600 (box lock)—it was this weapon that introduced me to the delights of the 24-inch-barrelled double—and I have never before, or since, handled an ultra-large bore that was better balanced or easier to handle.   I would never have believed that it weighed the 16 lb. at which it turned the scale had I not actually weighed it myself. It was only because I considered that 16 lb. was an unnecessary weight to carry around that I parted with my ·600 (Jeffery tells me that he is now building his ·600 to weigh but 14½ lb.).   The next Jeffery was a side lock ·400—a delightful little weapon ; and then a side lock

·450 No. 2 which was for some years my favourite rifle. Neither of these rifles was new—I only bought them because at that time I was still experimenting in order to find what I considered to be the ideal weapons—and the bores were badly corroded and worn. Had it not been for that fact, I might still have been using that same ·450 No. 2. Yet in spite of the disgraceful manner in which it had been ill-treated and neglected by its previous owner, it killed somewhere in the vicinity of 300 elephant for me.

If you deal with any firm mentioned in this book, and refrain from buying cheap weapons, you should have no cause for complaint. If you decide on any particular bore, other things being equal, it is usually advisable to go to the firm which makes a definite speciality of that particular bore—for instance : Westley Richards and the ·318 ; Jeffery and the ·333 ; Rigby and the ·350 magnum ; Purdey and the ·369 ; Holland and the ·375 magnum ; Jeffery and the ·404 ; and so on.

Auctor: You know, one cannot help remarking that you have had conspicuously little to say concerning the ·318. Umpteen men positively swear by it : reckon there's nothing like it under the sun ; but you don't appear to be particularly enamoured. Why ?

Lector: I see your point, and am glad you raised it ; but don't run away with the idea that I have no use for the ·318 ; on the contrary, I have the highest possible opinion of it provided it is kept in its place and not abused by being taken alone against dangerous game in thick cover. However, we'll give it a paragraph and see what we can find to say about it.

WESTLEY RICHARDS ·318

When this rifle was first introduced, during the early part of the present century, it was far ahead of all its contemporaries and instantly gained for itself an enviable reputation which it has worthily upheld. It took the big game hunting world by storm. Men soon got to know its amazing capabilities; but the trouble was that they did not discover its limitations equally as quickly—in fact, many of them refused to admit, or even consider the possibility, that it might have any limitations! However, with the introduction of Holland's ·375 magnum, men were compelled to realize that the ·318, wonderful little weapon and all as it undoubtedly was, was nevertheless *not* the last word in rifles. This, at the same time, in no way detracts from the excellence of the ·318 provided it is remembered that it was never intended for use against dangerous game at close quarters in thick cover. The makers, themselves, would be the last people in the world to recommend it for such work; in their catalogue and in their advertisements they only boost it for use against non-dangerous game: their ·425 is there for dangerous animals. The makers do not wish to see their ·318 used for dangerous animals because they know very well that if the habit is persisted in sooner or later someone will be disappointed, if not hurt or even killed—as has happened to several men in the past; and when these so-called " accidents " occur those who do not understand are apt to blame the rifle, in spite of the fact that the rifle is in no way to blame whatsoever. Let us listen-in to two of them chatting and yarning at sun-down over their whiskies and soda:

" That was damn bad luck about Brock, wasn't it ? "

" Why, what happened ? "

" What! Haven't you heard ? Why, the poor devil was pulled to pieces by an elephant only a couple of days ago ? "

" Good God ! That's the first I've heard of it. Poor old Charlie. What a hell of a pity. One of the decentest fellas you could wish to meet. But how did it happen ? "

" God knows. You know how difficult it is to get hold of the real facts in a case of this description; you know, yourself, how when tackling a herd of elephant in a dense matted tangle of bush it's pretty well a case of every man for himself, since you can't see what's happening other than in your immediate vicinity ; and I gather that his boys, other than his gunbearer, were all too busy looking after their own skins to be able to see much—can't say I blame them either !—when the stampede started. But so far as I can gather from his gunbearer, Charlie shot one of the herd and the remainder came crashing through the bush straight towards him. He could see nothing until one brute appeared right on top of him. He blazed off a shot, but it didn't appear to have any effect ; and the elephant, a large cow which had apparently charged the sound of the shot whilst the others were merely stampeding, got him down and proceeded to tear him in pieces. The gunbearer, who had been knocked down when the cow came through the bush, managed to get to his feet, pick up Charlie's second rifle, and put a shot from it into the beast. She then cleared off and fell dead a little way farther on."

" Good God ! Well I'm damn' sorry to hear that about old Charlie. But, you know, he's been asking for it for a hell of a long time."

" How do you mean, ' asking for it ' ? "

" He was using his ·318, I suppose ? "

" Of course. I don't think he ever used anything else. He had a second rifle—a ·450 I think it was—but I don't think he ever used it ; stuck to his ·318 and concentrated on, and specialized in, brain shots. A bit of an artist, he was, on brain shots."

" That's all very well ; but as I often tried to point out to him, if an elephant is practically on top of you a brain shot is an impossibility for any rifle under the sun. What the hell's the good of having a second rifle if you never use it ? I don't know whether you're interested in such matters or not, but I am, though I don't pretend to know much about it, and, you know, it seems to me that the 318 has gone off a lot recently."

" ' Gone off ' ? "

" Yes. It had a positively terrific reputation at one time : you could hardly meet a man who wasn't wildly enthusiastic about it—you could hardly get the blighters to speak of anything else but the ·318. But, you know, a hell of a lot of chaps seem to be getting themselves knocked about recently through using ·318's : there was Willis, chewed up by a lion only last month—he used a ·318 ; young Wright was killed by an elephant not long ago— he was using a ·318 ; and that fellow with the double-barrelled name who was so badly mauled by an elephant —he was a great believer in the ·318 ; and now here's Brock gone and got himself killed—another ·318 merchant. You see what I mean ? That's why I say that the ·318 seems to have gone off a lot."

Can't you just hear them ? Isn't it exactly how they talk ? But the ·318 has not " gone off ". Its ballistics have not been altered since it was introduced. It is merely that its devotees will not realize that it does not hit a sufficiently heavy blow to make it a safe weapon to take against dangerous game at close quarters. It will kill—but it will not always kill sufficiently quickly.

I have used the ·318 extensively. For some years I used a Westley Richards ·318 and swore by it ; but I always had a heavier weapon for use in thick cover because I realized the ·318's limitations. Always provided that there is the more powerful weapon at hand for use at close quarters, you could not wish for a better or more satisfactory general-purpose medium-bore than Westley Richards ·318 : it is a delightful little weapon to use, whilst its trajectory is as flat as you are ever likely to require in Africa. The diameter-to-weight ratio of its 250-grain bullet is probably better than that of any bullet on the market with the possible exception of the 300-grain bullet thrown by Jeffery's ·333. The combination of long, thin, parallel bullet of good weight and reasonably high velocity makes for very accurate shooting

and great depth of penetration ; whilst there is no tendency for the bullet to turn over or glance after entering
an animal's body.

Were I thinking of having Westley Richards build me
a new heavy double such as their ·476 and wanted a
magazine to go with it, I would almost certainly have him
build me a ·318 ; nor do I see the slightest reason for
supposing that I should ever live to regret it.

ORDERING AMMUNITION

Always order your ammuntion through your gunsmith
and do not buy it locally : you never can tell—until you
come to use it !—how long it may have been in stock.
All nitro powders deteriorate if kept unduly, and you
cannot afford to risk a misfire when tackling dangerous
game. If you only order your ammunition through
your gunsmith and have it soldered up in airtight packages
of not more than from 10 to 15 rounds, depending on the
extent to which you expect to be using it, you can rely
upon it being freshly loaded. If you are abroad and
expect to be doing a considerable amount of shooting,
order a special consignment through one of the manufacturers' agents ; you will get it very much cheaper this
way, and if you have it soldered up in packages of not more
than 50 rounds each it will keep indefinitely.

I have already, in a previous chapter, stressed the importance of giving every possible detail of the cartridges
when ordering a fresh consignment, so this will just be
a reminder. It is easy to imagine the disappointment, if
you are out in the " blue ", when you find that the cartridges do not fit the rifle. I was present on one never-
to-be-forgotten occasion when a man who had a double
·450 No. 2 opened a new consignment of ammunition and
found that some idiot of a dealer had sent him No. 2
musket cartridges ! They were of no more use to him
than ·450 revolver ammunition would have been. Of
course, the fault must have been his own in the first

instance for not giving full details of what he wanted—
he told me that in his order he had just stated that he
wanted 450 No. 2 cartridges, 480-grain bullet ; the No. 2
musket is also of ·450 calibre and throws a 480-grain
bullet—but the case is much smaller and of a different
shape, is loaded with black powder, whilst the bullet is
lead : Nitro Express ammunition was wanted, and metal-
covered bullets.

SINGLE TRIGGER

This, of course, concerns double rifles only. The only
double rifles that I have ever seen fitted with single-
trigger mechanism were Westley Richards's ; but I have
no doubt that other firms would give you single-trigger
mechanism on their best-quality rifles if you insisted on
it. The advantage of having only one trigger on a double
rifle is that you do not have to shift your hand to fire the
second barrel as you must if the weapon is fitted with two
triggers ; further, since the stock measurements are taken
from the front trigger if the weapon is fitted with two
triggers and since the front trigger is generally about
three-quarters of an inch in front of the back trigger, it
means that your rifle has two lenths of stock—one for
each trigger—and they cannot *both* be suitable. If a
quick second shot is called for, a man will seldom fire his
left barrel with quite the same degree of accuracy as he
fired his right if his rifle is fitted with two triggers :
simply because he has had to shift his hand and the stock
is now three-quarters of an inch too short for him in addition to the fact that he may not have been able to get quite
so comfortable a grip. With but one trigger, you get
the same length of stock with both barrels and do not
have to move your hand : the second shot can be fired
with exactly the same degree of accuracy as the first and
considerably quicker than it could with two triggers. I
admit, it is mighty seldom that it is necessary to fire the
second shot so rapidly on the heels of the first, but it does

sometimes help enormously in very thick bush when you only get a fleeting glimpse of the vital spot on some beast as it passes across a small gap in the foliage after the first shot has been fired. I am perfectly certain that on a number of occasions I was able to bag a second elephant, rhino, or buffalo, as the case might be, when using Westley Richards One-Trigger mechanism which I would not have had a hope of bagging had my rifle been fitted with two triggers. But personally I consider that the greatest advantage of all conferred by the single-trigger is the elimination of the necessity for moving the hand ; particularly do I find it so when closing a herd of buffalo in long grass when you cannot tell until the very last moment which barrel you will want to fire first—the right with its solid bullet, or the left with its soft-nosed.

It is sometimes urged that single-trigger mechanism, by being complicated, must detract from the reliability of the weapon on the grounds that the more complications there are the greater likelihood there must be of something going wrong. But I cannot see the force of that argument or admit its validity. Since exactly the same mechanism is fitted in best-quality shot-guns which may be called upon to fire anything up to ten thousand or more cartridges a year, and will stand this incessant hammering year after year without breaking down, what earthly reason is there to suppose that it will not stand up to the very few hundred cartridges a year that it will be asked to fire when fitted in a rifle ? Even a professional hunter will seldom fire more than from 200 to 300 cartridges a year through any one of his rifles. In other words, the mechanism in a shot-gun may be called upon to stand up to more work in one year than in the whole lifetime of a rifle (assuming that the latter was not fitted with a new pair of barrels when the original pair were worn out). To condemn the mechanism simply because it is more complicated than double triggers is, in my opinion, unreasonable : side locks are more complicated than box locks, but that does not detract from their reliability and the great majority of gunsmiths fit their best-quality guns and rifles with side locks ; hammerless actions are more complicated than hammer actions, but their experience has shown gunsmiths how to build hammerless ejector actions which are every bit as reliable as hammer actions, if not even more so (for instance, it is practically unknown for the discharge of one barrel of a hammerless action to jar off the other barrel, but this was a great failing on powerful double-hammer rifles— so much so, in fact, that on large bores it was necessary to leave the second hammer at half-cock until after the first barrel had been fired).

I used a Westley Richards double ·577 Nitro Express for some considerable time with the utmost satisfaction and have never since felt really happy with two triggers —I am determined that my next double rifle shall have but the one trigger. Sutherland, the first man to shoot 1,000 elephant, used and swore by Westley Richards One-Trigger mechanism on his pair of double ·577's ; he would hardly have done so had he not found it eminently satisfactory.

DOUBLE-PULL TRIGGERS

This refers to magazine rifles only. I cannot under-stand why gunsmiths almost invariably fit double-pull triggers on their magazine rifles : I cannot see the object of a double-pull trigger. But I know that it is a great mistake to have a magazine rifle fitted with a double-pull trigger if you also use a double rifle ; because no double rifle is fitted with a double-pull trigger, and if you have been using your magazine rifle extensively and then change to the double you will be very apt to fire your first shot before you intend to, through automatically " taking up the slack ", or tightening your finger to take up the first pull as you had to do on the magazine. You should insist on your magazine being fitted with a single-pull trigger.

HAIR TRIGGERS

I certainly do not recommend these for ordinary shooting. If you permit yourself to become accustomed to a hair trigger when taking deliberate shots, when called upon to take a quick shot you will not have time in which to snick back the hindermost trigger to set the hair trigger mechanism and now, having become accustomed to a very light pull, will find the front trigger impossibly heavy and the result will be that you will almost inevitably " pull off " your target. The only type of shooting in Africa for which I like a hair trigger is when trying to get a shot at a very shy hippo which has been shot at before. For long periods—perhaps anything from twenty minutes to half an hour—he will only raise his nostrils above the surface : it is no use shooting at those ; but sooner or later he will expose the top of his head to have a look around and see if the coast is clear. This is your chance ; but since he will only expose a vital spot for a matter of a couple of seconds or so, and since you may have been lying on your aim for a long, long time waiting for him, you will almost certainly " yank " at your trigger in an effort to get the shot off in time. A hair trigger helps enormously here : in fact, with a 'scope sight and a hair trigger you can count that hippo as yours provided he does not clear off without giving you a shot at all; whereas, with open or even aperture sights and an ordinary trigger he will be pretty safe no matter how fine a marksman may be behind the rifle, because the man's eye will become so tired and strained aiming with the ordinary sights.

But if you decide to have a hair trigger, you must insist on the front, or firing, trigger having a perfectly normal pull. On every rifle fitted with a hair trigger that I have ever handled the pull of the front trigger was so impossibly heavy that nobody could shoot accurately with it without setting the hair trigger mechanism. If you have a normal pull for the front trigger you can use it for all ordinary shooting, and keep the hair trigger for exceptional occasions : do not get into the habit of using the hair trigger when it is not necessary. In no circumstances should you ever attempt to take a running shot with the hair trigger mechanism in action.

RECOIL PADS

I strongly recommend these to be fitted to all guns and rifles (other than miniatures) for use in the tropics where practically all shooting takes place in shirt sleeves. Although in the excitement of the moment you may not feel any recoil at all, a very severe recoil can have most unpleasant after effects ; if you are firing from an awkward position a rifle which normally appears to have no recoil whatever can make itself felt on occasions, and a tenderness about the shoulder may very easily make you flinch slightly next day and this can have but one result. If you are only on a visit to the tropics and do not want to have the stock of your gun shortened to accommodate a recoil pad, a slip-on pad will be perfectly satisfactory ; the rifles should be fitted with permanent pads.

USING RESTS

Time and again in Africa I have heard men scorning rests and averring that they are unsporting. How *can* a rest be considered " unsporting " when it so indubitably assists you to place your shots accurately and, therefore, to kill cleanly ? Personally, I make no bones about it— I invariably use a rest when the conditions permit, as also do I use the sling round my left arm. But I have noticed more than once that those selfsame men who, when seated in comfortable armchairs on the verandah, had scorned the use of a rest are themselves the first to look for a convenient tree or anthill when it actually comes to taking a shot !

Never rest your rifle on anything hard such as a branch of a tree or rock when about to fire. The rifle will jump away from the hard rest and throw the shot high. It is best to rest the rifle against the side of the tree, or rest the hand which holds the barrel on the rock. In the open when the grass is short I kneel down and steady the muzzle of the rifle against the side of my tracker's thigh. In long grass, if there is no convenient tree, then I either use the top of his head or, if he is a very tall lad, his shoulder. Of course, when shooting at close ranges a rest is not necessary, and, in snap-shots, is out of the question. Believe me, there are mighty few men who, having been tramping for several hours in the sweltering heat, could take a standing shot, without using a rest, at an animal 200 yards away, and bring off a clean kill.

LOADING MAGAZINE RIFLES

Gunmakers with, to the best of my knowledge, but one exception, all recommend you to charge the magazine of your rifle and then slip an extra round into the chamber. Of course, they can hardly be blamed for doing so because in all probability they have never hunted dangerous game and therefore cannot be expected to visualize the consequences which might ensue if this practice is adopted. To my mind it is asking for trouble ; yet the vast majority of sportsmen in Africa invariably do it. That one exception to whom I have referred is John Rigby. He in his catalogue emphasizes the importance of always loading from the magazine platform, and I most emphatically agree with him ; although he omits to give his reasons. But my reasons for maintaining that the capacity of a magazine rifle should be the capacity of its magazine and of its magazine only, are as follows :

If you use a magazine rifle with, say, a four-shot magazine and are in the habit of slipping a fifth cartridge into the chamber after fully charging the magazine, then you will inevitably come to think, subconsciously, in terms of four shots in reserve after you have fired the first. But, if you find yourself surrounded by a large herd of elephant or buffalo in long grass or thick bush, or possibly have open fire on a large troop of lion and, having fired two or three rounds or more, then want to reload your rifle, the temptation to slip that extra round up the spout will be almost irresistible. If you are in the act of doing so and suddenly find a portion of the herd taking it into their heads to stampede towards you, or possibly find yourself being charged, then in your hurry to get the rifle ready for action you will be running a very grave risk of giving yourself a dangerous jam at a critical moment. And that jam might have very serious, even disastrous, consequences for you—or, what is far more important, for your tracker and gunbearer. If, on the other hand, you realize the possibility of such a jam occurring should you be hurried, and refrain from slipping that extra round up the spout, then you will now have one round less in reserve than the number upon which you have, subconsciously, come to rely. In the excitement of, quite possibly, defending your life you may omit to keep count of the number of rounds that you have fired, and may also, quite easily under the circumstances, forget that you now have one round less than usual in the rifle. The result being that you may find yourself snapping an empty rifle in a vain endeavour to stop a charging elephant or lion.

But if you had always been in the habit of just charging the magazine and then closing the bolt, you will subconsciously come to think in terms of the magazine's capacity only. And then there would be no fear of ever giving yourself a dangerous jam, nor would there be any risk of forgetting the number of rounds that you have fired. Because, although you may not consciously be counting them, nevertheless, subconsciously, you are ; and having fired the last cartridge in the rifle, you will automatically lower the butt from your shoulder and prepare to recharge the magazine. You will not be wasting precious seconds in futile snapping of empty weapons !

If you have been accustomed to slip that extra round up the spout and now cease doing so, just at first you may feel that you are very poorly armed, but you will very soon become accustomed to it and will find that four quick shots are ample. If you think that you could not feel really happy without the five, well—your gunsmith will always be willing to give you a slightly larger magazine if you really want it.

The capacity of the magazine should always be considered as the capacity of the rifle. Let nothing induce you to get into the habit of slipping that extra round up the spout.

CARRYING MAGAZINE RIFLES

Throughout the preceding chapters, which were originally written a considerable time ago, I have rather condemned the magazine rifle for certain types of hunting, principally because it cannot be swung into action as quickly as can a double, and I still contend that the double is to be preferred for those particular types of hunting because of its shortness, handiness, greater reliability and infinitely better balance. Nevertheless, it is only fair to the magazine to admit that as a result of considerable experimenting I find that there is a method of carrying this type of weapon which is perfectly safe and yet, at the same time, permits of a shot being got off with the very minimum of delay. Doubtless magazine enthusiasts will have known of it long ago ; but for the benefit of those who may not, I mention it for what it is worth.

You carry the rifle with the finger-piece of the safety in the vertical position instead of over to the right. In this position the rifle cannot be fired, so that there is no fear of blowing your tracker's head off. If a sudden chance is offered, or a quick shot required to stop an unexpected charge, your thumb, lying alongside the right-hand side of the safety, just presses sideways, the safety flops over to the firing position on the left and the thumb follows it and gets into the normal position on the grip. With a little practice this operation can be performed quite easily and quickly and enables the shot to be got off with the minimum of delay—far more quickly than if the safety is carried in the normal position on the right of the action. If carried as I suggest, the safety can be pressed down into the firing position whilst the rifle is actually on its way up to the shoulder, and therefore compares very favourably with the double ; though I should always recommend the double in preference to the magazine for these particular types of hunting because of the better balance, the greater handiness owing to its shortness, and the more certain reliability.

ORDERING RIFLES

A very important point which is frequently overlooked is the absolute necessity for having your rifles built as nearly as possible alike. There is then no feeling of strangeness when changing from one to another for a different type of hunting. Whenever possible have all your magazine rifles built by the one firm, all with the same magazine capacity, and all with exactly the same type of trigger and identical trigger pulls ; and all your doubles also built by the one firm, either the same or another, it matters not. But the great thing is to have them all with the same type of action, and all details such as safeties, triggers, top-lever, etc., identical—or at least all working in an identical manner.

To show the danger of having, for instance, two double rifles with widely different types of action, the following incident is, I think, worth mentioning :

That German hunter to whom I have previously referred had two best-quality British-built doubles, bought second-hand from, I think, their makers. He shot from the left shoulder. Now his Evans ·450 had been built for a right-handed man, and the top lever worked in the normal way—that is, out to the right ; but his Holland ·465 " Royal " had either been built for a left-handed man, or else he had had it altered when he bought it, because its top lever worked towards the left— as it should do for a man who shoots from his left shoulder. Of course, he did not take both weapons out when actually hunting, but kept one in reserve in case of the other meeting with an accident—a possibility which cannot be ignored by the professional hunter. And although it was unwise to have two weapons with such widely differing actions, it would not have been so bad if " M " had not gaily used them alternately : sometimes month and month about, sometimes week and week about.

I remember that we were camped close to one another in a district in which there were ample elephant for two men. I prefer to hunt alone and keep my own camp, but we would usually foregather in the evening for a " sun-downer " and a chat over the day's hunt. " M " being extremely enthusiastic and knowing far more about ballistics than I did, we frequently discussed rifles. I asked him once if he did not think that he was asking for trouble by using his doubles alternately, bearing in mind their widely different actions. But he replied that he never forgot. Yet it was only the following morning when he *did* forget, and had a very narrow escape in consequence. He had followed a mixed herd of bulls and cows into a very dense patch of bush. He dropped a nice young bull which was standing on his half-left with a side brain shot and was immediately attacked by a cow which had been standing just beside him, behind a very thick bush, on his half-right. He wheeled round and blazed upwards into her face ; and the bullet, by a stroke of luck, took her in the eye and, passing up the eye socket, found the brain, killing her instantly. " M " then lowered the butt of the rifle from his shoulder with the intention of reloading, when he heard a portion of the herd stampeding straight towards him. He wrenched

13

at the top lever of his rifle, but found that it had, apparently, jammed ; and he and his tracker and gunbearer had to run for it.   Fortunately for them, there was a large baobab tree only a few paces away, and they just, and only just, managed to get behind it before the panic-stricken herd crashed past on both sides.   " M " then examined his rifle to see what had caused it to jam ; but there was nothing the matter with it at all—it was just that in the excitement of the moment he had forgotten which weapon he was handling and had been endeavouring to force the top lever out in the wrong direction !

OBJECTION TO VERY LIGHT RIFLES

Auctor :   In view of the positive mania there is, and always has been, in Africa for very light rifles, would you mind explaining why you dislike them.   I fully appreciate the necessity for a powerful rifle when tackling the big fellows in the thick cover ; but all hunting does not take place in the thick stuff.   And since in more open country there is not the same risk of stubbing your toe on an animal before you see him, provided the bullet thrown is not so light that it will disintegrate on impact, why should not a light rifle prove perfectly satisfactory ? It would be very much easier to carry than a heavier weapon.

Lector :   Certainly, it would ;   and a walking-stick would be even easier still to carry and of greater help to you if you were tired.   But a walking-stick would not be of much use to you if you wanted to shoot anything, and I contend that a featherweight rifle will not be of much more service to you than a stick when you are dog-tired at the end of a long hard day.   Such a weapon absolutely refuses to keep still if you happen to be fatigued—and you are often fatigued in the African bush.   At six o'clock in the morning you may be able to place your shots beautifully accurately with the little rifle ; but just see what sort of a performance you will put up at six

o'clock in the evening with the same weapon after tramping all day in the sweltering heat ! Suppose it is getting
along towards sun-down and you are on your way back
to camp when you are offered the chance of a lifetime :
do what you will, that little, light rifle will not settle
down steadily in your hand ; finally, with the muzzle
of the rifle describing circles all over the animal, you
in desperation yank at the trigger and hope for the best,
and away goes your fine trophy. The small bullet
means a small entrance hole to the wound—assuming
that you have hit the animal at all—and this in turn
means little or no blood spoor ; the light is failing, you
cannot follow far ; eventually you are obliged to give up
the chase and plod wearily on with yet another heart-
breaking disappointment to round off a disappointing
day. Had you used a heavier rifle, it would have settled
down much more steadily in your hand and therefore
permitted of a more accurately placed bullet ; in addition
to which the larger bullet would have caused a more
reliable blood spoor and done more damage even if it had
failed to kill outright. If you are hunting in open
country, there is not the same necessity for you to carry
the rifle yourself since you can see the game sooner :
there is little or no likelihood of your wanting to take a
snap-shot. Personally, I like my rifles to weigh from
$9\frac{1}{2}$ lb. to $10\frac{1}{2}$ lb. and would not care to use a rifle weighing
less than $8\frac{1}{2}$ lb.

Auctor : Yes, but does the man who does a fair
amount of shooting not find that his ammunition bill
mounts up rather alarmingly if he uses these more
powerful weapons for non-dangerous game ?

Lector : Ammunition forms a comparatively small
item in even a professional hunter's total expense sheet.
Besides, before ever you come to the question of ammunition, there is the cost of that small rifle to be considered ; and there is seldom any difference worth
mentioning in the cost of different calibres. Don't forget

that the price of that rifle must be added to the price
of the ammunition if a fair comparison is to be made.
But even apart from that, experience has shown that
frequently two, three, or even more shots must be fired
from those low-powered rifles to effect a kill where one
shot from a more powerful weapon would be sufficient.
Accordingly, since the ammunition for the more powerful weapons does certainly not cost two or three times the
amount of the other, it will usually be found that the
more powerful stuff actually works out cheaper in the
long run—quite apart from the cost of the light rifle.

SIDE LOCK *v.* BOX LOCK

Auctor :   Precisely what advantage, if any, has the side
lock over the box lock ?   I notice that practically all
gunsmiths fit their best-quality double rifles with side
locks, and they certainly have a more imposing appear-
ance and give greater scope to the engraver than the box
lock ; but are they really any better ?   And if so, in what
way ?

Lector :   Owing to its design, which necessitates less of
the action having to be cut away to accommodate the
limbs, the side-lock action is stronger than the ordinary
Anson & Deeley box lock which was originally introduced
by Westley Richards as the first hammerless action.
But Westley Richards's modern improvements on that
original design which permits of the separate locks being
detached by hand, leaves this action as made by him
every bit as strong as any side lock action.   A further
advantage of the side lock over the ordinary box lock is
that the design permits of a more perfect trigger release ;
though here again Westley Richards's hand-detachable
locks have just as perfect a trigger release as any side lock.

The box lock has less than half the number of moving
parts required in the side lock, and since machine work
can be used satisfactorily to a greater extent in its manu-
facture it is possible to build a box-lock weapon and sell it

at a lower price than an equally good side-lock weapon. The principal disadvantage of the box lock is that you cannot examine it as you can the side lock to see that any moisture that may have got in is properly dried out and the lock cleaned and oiled ; but to offset this, there is the fact that the box lock is more naturally waterproof than the side lock. Nevertheless, I must say that I like to be able to satisfy myself absolutely concerning the inner comfort of the locks on all my rifles, particularly those which are taken against dangerous game—rust is insidious stuff ; however, it is only fair to admit that I have never had a box lock let me down : I have never even heard of the locks of a good rifle breaking down. Westley Richards's hand-detachable box locks are undoubtedly the simplest and most convenient on the market ; though Holland's hand-detachable side locks run them close for convenience (this pattern is now fitted by several other firms).

Some men declare that they can see no advantage in hand-detachable locks ; but to me the advantage is very real. Human nature being what it is, locks which require turnscrews to remove them will not be removed and examined anything like so often as will locks which can be removed by hand without any tools whatever being needed. In wet weather your locks should be examined frequently : it is astonishing how easily and how quickly rust *can*, and sometimes will, form. Besides, it is very easy to burr the heads of the screws in the lock plates if you are tired, and if you succeed in making a bad mess of one of them you may cease bothering about it and just let the locks take pot luck in future.

SINGLE-BARRELLED SINGLE-LOADERS

Auctor : I don't know whether you have forgotten or not, but a long time ago you promised to say something about single-loaders.

Lector : Yes, and I have quite a lot to say about them

too ; because, in my humble opinion, magazine rifles should be banned from the realms of sport. They were invented for military purposes and should be left solely and entirely in the hands of the military. There is a psychological factor which arises when a man knows that he has three or four quick shots in immediate reserve. I have seen it again and again in Africa, and have no doubt that it is to be seen elsewhere also though possibly not to the same extent since there is not the same quantity of game in other countries. But in Africa, if the game do not all stampede on the heels of the first shot, the man thinks to himself that here is a fine opportunity to make a big bag. His second shot is somewhat rushed in the hope of getting a third ; and his third and fourth are probably wildly ripped off from the magazine as the remainder of the herd clears off. The result is that for the one animal possibly killed there may be two or three wounded. Although he may succeed in finding and finishing off one of those wounded ; what chance has he of doing so with them all ? Following up that wounded one may take him miles away from where the others are ; he will almost certainly be too tired eventually to follow up each and all of them. Lions in particular seem to affect men in this way.

But if he had been using a single-loader, each and every shot would have been carefully placed because there would have been no incentive to rush it, since there was nothing in immediate reserve and it is improbable that the animals will give another chance. I cannot see why a man should *want* to make a big bag at a " sitting " ; and even if he does, my own experience is—and I write as a professional who has all too frequently to shoot for quantity rather than quality—that if the gods are on your side that day and intend to give you several beasts, you will kill them with a single-loader every bit as easily as ever you would with a magazine, and with a far greater degree of confidence, simply because each shot is fired as though it was the first and last—the only one for which you can reasonably hope, and therefore deserving of the utmost care in the firing of it.

When I first started hunting, I used nothing but doubles and singles. Later, when I decided to experiment with magazines, I used only to load two cartridges into them so as to avoid any possibility of succumbing to the temptation mentioned above. I am firmly convinced that if the Governments concerned would prohibit the use of magazine rifles and insist that all rifles, other than heavy, powerful weapons obviously intended for use against dangerous game at close quarters, be fitted with telescope sights, it would be the greatest step forward towards genuine Game Preservation that has ever been taken at one stride. I am sure that it is no exaggeration to say that there must be literally thousands of animals needlessly wounded throughout the big game hunting world every year through the use of magazine rifles and open sights, and which would not have been so wounded had 'scope-sighted single-loaders been used.

The falling block single-loader has one of the very best actions that has ever been designed : strong, simple, silent, certain in use, and absolutely reliable. Its one and only weak point is the extractor. The design does not lend itself to much leverage being available for primary extraction, and if the chamber is badly worn or pitted with rust it may fail to dislodge the fired shell. But that is the fault of the owner for permitting rust to form in the chamber. If a very high-pressure cartridge is used it may expand to such an extent that it also will stick in even a clean chamber ; but there are plenty of equally good cartridges developing lower chamber pressures, so why not use some of them ? If magazine rifles were prohibited in sport, the combined brains of the gun trade in all countries manufacturing sporting rifles would be brought to bear on this question of primary extraction, and there cannot be the slightest doubt that in a very short time some improvement or modification of the existing action would be discovered which would remove once and for all the bugbear of a jammed shell and render the extraction as sure and as certain as it is on double rifles.

An additional advantage which would appear if magazines were banned is that many men who now use magazine rifles would buy doubles. This increase in the demand for doubles would mean that more of the parts could be cut out in the rough state, and this would reduce the overhead costs which in turn would mean that double rifles could be sold at a somewhat lower price.

'SCOPE SIGHTS FOR RUNNING SHOTS

Auctor : Your mention of a 'scope-sighted single-loader reminds me of a question I wanted to ask you. How does a properly mounted 'scope sight pan out if you want to take a shot at a running animal ? How does it compare with, say, a peep-sight ? I seem to remember somebody saying that a 'scope sight was slow for running shots.

Lector : As I have already stated, I belong to that school which never attempts to press trigger until it can clearly see its way to make a kill. In my early days I several times attempted what appeared to be very easy shots at running animals, with both open and aperture sights (I don't, of course, mean open and aperture sights used together at the same time), but the result was invariably the same : I hit the animals too far back. Pick up any book on African big game hunting and read on until the author describes how he took a running shot at a lion or other beast, and how the lion " acknowledged the bullet with a grunt of rage " but carried on, and then how a subsequent examination of the lion showed that " my first shot had taken him too far back ". It is always the same ; and the explanation is to be found in the fact that, with ordinary iron sights, a man will give a final glance at the sights the instant before he squeezes the trigger just to make absolutely certain that they are as he wants them and this momentarily taking his eye off his target will inevitably cause a slight check in the swing of the rifle which will cause the bullet to hit the animal too far back. I know that there are men who try to intercept an animal by aiming at a given point ahead of him and then firing the instant they think he is close enough ; but you will never kill by such a method other than by a fluke. The only method of shooting a moving target with any degree of certainty whatsoever is to swing with the target and fire without checking the movement of the muzzles until after the trigger has been pressed. The slightest check in the swing of the muzzles will mean a miss behind in the case of a bird, and a hit too far back in the case of an animal. The greatest exponents of the shot-gun will tell you that checking the swing is one of the greatest difficulties that they have to overcome and that they frequently miss a bird in spite of all their practice through this very fault ; so what hope has the big game shot who gets no practice at all, as you might say, since running shots are not frequent ?

For years, after those early disappointments, I never attempted to shoot a running beast other, perhaps, than an elephant stampeding directly across my front at very close range. But after I took to using low-powered, low-mounted telescope sights I found that it was almost as easy to hit and kill a running animal as it was a stationary one. Because with a 'scope sight there is no taking your eye off the target for a last glance at the sights, since the aiming post of the graticule is superimposed on the part of the animal that you want to hit and in constant focus with it. Just as there is no tendency to check the swing of your binoculars when following the fortunes of your favourite in a steeplechase, so also will you find it when taking a running shot with a properly mounted 'scope sight. You have only to place the graticule well forward on the animal's shoulder, keep it there as you swing with him, and press the trigger when you feel like it.

Only this morning, I bagged five buffalo with a 'scope-sighted ·375 magnum : the first, a big bull, standing, and the remainder as the herd stampeded across my front. With open or aperture sights I should not have attempted it : I should have been satisfied with the first, and then followed up the herd and bagged another, after which I should have done the same thing again and continued doing so until I had got my five. It might have taken me half a day to kill them all ; whereas, with 'scope sight, I bagged all five in about half a minute.

EXPANDING BULLETS

Auctor : I wish you would give us your views on expanding bullets. Out of the umpteen varieties obtainable, which do you consider the best ? I have frequently noticed in the correspondence columns of the sporting journals that a man lauds to the skies one type of bullet which he has found satisfactory, and then, only perhaps a week later, somebody else is equally emphatic in condemning that very same bullet fired from an identical rifle. What is the earnest seeker after knowledge to do in the case of such contradictory reports ?

Lector : From the very fact that there are so many different patterns available, it is surely obvious that there is no such thing as an ideal expanding bullet. If there was, then it, and it only, would be manufactured, since there would be no demand for anything else. It is almost invariably the case that when a man condemns any particular type of expanding bullet he does so in general terms and without any reference whatsoever to either the weight of the bullet or the weight of animal against which it was used. If an expanding bullet is intended for use against some of the heavier varieties of game, it will be designed for penetration combined with expansion. Naturally, then, such a bullet would be little if any better than a solid when used on one of the lighter animals, since it would not encounter sufficient resistance to cause it to set up before it had passed clean through that little animal's body. In exactly the same way, if a bullet is designed for the rapid expansion necessary for the lighter varieties of soft-skinned game, it will blow to pieces on striking a bone on one of the heavier varieties. A sense of proportion must be maintained and a suitable weight of bullet chosen for the weight of animal most likely to be shot.

With regard to the different patterns of expanding bullet : here again common sense must be brought to bear and a thought given to the weight of animal it is desired to shoot. To a very great extent this question of bullet weight and pattern is mixed up with the choice of calibres ; but if only the one rifle is to be used for all types of shooting, well—three different weights of bullet are obtainable for the ·375 magnum, because the designers realized the necessity for such in view of the widely differing weights of animal that might be shot, as also did they realize that it was necessary that all these different weights should be of different patterns : some being of a type which will expand more readily than others. Nevertheless, irrespective of the pattern of bullet, by far the most important consideration is its weight ; because even a fairly light bullet of a type that does not expand too readily might be better on occasions than an appreciably heavier bullet of a type that expands very easily. For instance, I should very much rather tackle buffalo with a Westley Richards's round-capped or even plain soft-nosed 250-grain bullet from a ·318 than I would with a copper-pointed 300-grain bullet from a ·404 ; the reason being that the copper-pointed type of bullet is intended for rapid expansion, and if the expansion is too rapid it will blow to pieces.

The principal types of expanding bullet are as follows :

(1) Westley Richards's round-capped .   slow expansion.
(2) Soft-nose—lead barely showing at
    the tip .   .   .   .   .   slow expansion.
(3) Soft-nose—plenty of lead showing   normal expansion.
(4) Soft-nose split .   .   .   .   rapid expansion.
(5) Copper-pointed .   .   .   .   very rapid expansion.
(6) Westley Richards's " L.T." pointed
    capped .   .   .   .   .   instantaneous expansion.

It is absurd to suggest, as do some men who use the old black powder ·500 and ·577 Expresses with their solid lead bullets for tiger shooting in India, that no metal-covered expanding bullet will do other than disintegrate on hitting a tiger.   I have never hunted in India ; but for the purposes of this discussion a lion may be considered as being the same as a tiger, and I have had ample experience of shooting lion.   If some little featherweight bullet of, perhaps, 140 grains or so with a very high striking velocity is used, of course it will blow to pieces on so comparatively massive an animal as a lion ; but when bullets ranging from 480 to 520 grains are used, most men, both in India as well as in Africa, generally prefer to use the soft-nose split pattern so as to ensure the bullet setting up on so comparatively lightly-boned animals as lion and tiger instantly become when bullets of these weights are on the *tapis*.   (The combination I prefer for lion is a soft-nose split in the right barrel for broadside shots, and a plain soft-nose with plenty of lead showing in the left barrel for frontal shots.)   To show the absurdity of stating that *any* soft-nosed metal-covered bullet will blow to pieces if it hits even a rib on such animals as lion or tiger, the very heaviest of which do not weigh more than from 600 to 700 lb and generally very much less (the heaviest lion on record weighed some 720 or 730 lb. an hour or so after being shot ; but the average would probably work out at about 500 lb. or thereabouts—experienced *shikaris* in India state that the average weight of tigers is probably from 425 to 435 lb.) I might just mention that during the four and a half months that I was amongst them last year, I shot ninety-two buffalo with soft-nose (480-grain) bullets, plenty of lead showing at the nose, from my ·450 No. 2. Ninety-one of these I killed ; one got away from me with a broken fore-leg owing to my misjudging his height in the grass and aiming a trifle too low. Well now, since African buffalo average close on a ton—big bulls must weigh well over a ton—and since these plain soft-nose bullets behaved so splendidly on them, it's manifestly absurd to suggest that the same bullets would disintegrate on animals weighing only one-quarter as much.

It is quite impossible to recommend any particular pattern of expanding bullet without first knowing what weight of bullet is being considered and what weight of animal it is intended to shoot with it.

Auctor : What do you think of Westley Richards's capped bullets ? They had a tremendous vogue when they first came out and many men still swear by them, others, however, do not.

Lector : I am one of those who do. When they were first introduced they were obtainable for practically every calibre on the market at that time ; subsequently, however, other calibres were introduced for which they are not available. The reason why some men dislike them is that they have only used the " L.T." pointed hollow-capped pattern, generally in a light rifle, and naturally found that it lacked penetration when used against some of the heavier animals. It was never intended for such work. If you examine the two patterns, the " L.T." pointed-capped and the round-capped, you will see that they are of entirely different design. See them in section, and the difference is immediately apparent—if you cannot see them elsewhere in section, you should get hold of Westley Richards's catalogue : you will find them in it. The pointed cap is hollow, and the hollow extends into the nose of the bullet ; this means that it *must* set up on impact irrespective of whether or not it hits a bone. Accordingly, if a fairly light bullet of this type is used on a fairly heavy animal it will probably fail to penetrate sufficiently—but that is not the fault of the bullet ; it is the fault of the man who uses the wrong pattern. The round-capped bullet is quite different. It more closely resembles a soft-nose bullet with an exceptional amount of lead showing at the nose ; the cap is then placed over the exposed lead so as to protect it and prevent the bullet expanding too soon. It is splendidly effective on all the heavier varieties of game, having excellent penetration.

An additional advantage claimed by the inventor is that these capped bullets will not jam in magazine rifles, as many men—principally those who use cheap Continental weapons—complain happens with the ordinary soft-nose bullet (I have never known this happen with a good-quality rifle, and suspect that faulty chambering is probably to blame) owing to the soft exposed lead tending to " nick " and catch on the entrance to the chamber.

Provided that the more suitable of the two patterns is chosen, and which is the more suitable depends entirely on the weight of bullet and the weight of animal, then Westley Richards's capped bullets will be found to be splendidly effective on all animals for which expanding bullets are required. So much so, in fact, that if a choice is being made between two rifles of approximately the same power and you find it difficult to decide which one to buy, if Westley Richards's capped bullets are available for one and not for the other I should be inclined to advise you to let that be the deciding factor.

DOUBLES FOR RIMLESS CARTRIDGES

Auctor : Have you ever used a double firing rimless cartridges as fired in magazine rifles ? Are they equally as reliable as those firing flanged cartridges ?

Lector : No, I have never actually used one myself ; but I know of several men, amateurs, who use them, and they appear to be perfectly satisfied. It is generally considered that on account of the difficulties in designing suitable extractors for rimless cartridges, they do not function as well as with flanged cartridges. This is what gunsmiths and various other people will tell you. But Westley Richards has been building double rifles for rimless cartridges for many years, and it is inconceivable that a firm having Westley Richards's enviable reputation would build and continue to build costly best-quality double rifles of any type which were not one hundred per cent satisfactory. He has, of course, his own patent extractor mechanism which he claims functions as perfectly with rimless cartridges as it does with flanged cartridges. Although, as I say, I have never as yet had an opportunity of trying out such a weapon, I know that if somebody was to present me with one now I should use it with every confidence.

Auctor : But what precisely is the object of having a double firing magazine rifle ammunition ?

Lector : Just that it enables you to have both double and magazine handling the same ammunition, which is a great boon in that it saves you having to bother about different kinds of cartridges for both of which you will probably be wanting at least two different kinds of bullet. I have often thought that a battery consisting of an open-sighted double ·425 (26-inch barrels) and a 'scope-sighted ·425 magazine (25-inch barrel) would take an immense amount of beating for general all-round work amongst dangerous game, and am seriously considering just such a battery when it is possible for me to order a new one.

VERTICAL STANDARD ON ALL-ROUND RIFLE

Auctor : By the way, in your chapter on sighting you recommend that the standard backsight should be made so that it slopes towards the muzzles as this makes it more suitable for use in the bad light found in heavy forest. But what about an all-round rifle ?   It will not be always used in heavy forest, and a sight sloping towards the muzzles will undoubtedly dazzle sometimes in open country and possibly lose you the trophy of a lifetime. What do you suggest ?

Lector : A quickly-detachable 'scope sight, of course.

Auctor : Yes ; but supposing the man simply cannot rise to the price of a 'scope.

Lector : Well, if the rifle was being built for me I should certainly have it sighted in the most suitable manner for use in thick cover if it was sometimes to be used there, because it might easily develop into a matter of life and death.   There is not the same likelihood of such contingencies arising in the open, and if they do the animals must of necessity be close when the pattern of sight is of little moment.   However, if the weapon is to be used considerably in open country with open sights, I should imagine that a vertical backsight would be the best compromise : it would not be likely to dazzle in the open unless the sun was very close to the horizon behind you, whilst it is not too bad in heavy forest.   Yes, the all-round rifle should be fitted with a vertical standard backsight if a 'scope sight is not going to be used when in open country.

BARREL LENGTH

Auctor : Unless I've misread you, I gather that in your opinion the question of barrel length is of minor importance at the ranges at which sporting rifles are normally used.

Lector : Yes, when normal lengths of barrel are being considered.   Nowadays, sporting rifles are rarely built with barrels of more than 26 inches in length other than to special order by some idiot who thinks that he will be able to shoot more accurately with 28-inch barrels.   The customary length is anything from 24 inches to 26 inches for both doubles and magazines, and for all practical purposes of sport there is nothing to choose between them from the point of view of killing power. As I have explained in the chapter dealing with elephant rifles, I gave not a little thought to this question of barrel length in the days when I was experimenting, and used some of the cartridges in several different lengths of barrel to test the effect. For instance, I have used two different ·465's : one with 26-inch barrels and the other with 24's ; I have also used four different ·450 No. 2's : one with 28-inch barrels, another with 26-inch barrels and yet two others both fitted with 24-inch barrels. And I can honestly state that I never noticed the slightest difference in the killing-power of the weapons.

The length of barrel with which you have your rifles built is entirely a matter of personal preference : some men like shorter barrels than others ; but I think that, as with shot-guns, the length of the barrel should bear some relation to the length of stock. For instance, a very tall man who requires an exceptionally long stock would probably like somewhat longer barrels than would a small man whose rifle would be fitted with a very much shorter stock. Personally, after trying all lengths, I find that I prefer 25-inch and 26-inch barrels, and that these lengths give me the best balance.

PLEA TO GUNSMITHS

I should like to appeal to gunsmiths to cease building rifles for out-of-date cartridges. At the present time there are more than 120 different rifle cartridges manufactured in England as well as a number of others that are only obtainable abroad. The vast majority of these are obsolete—obsolete, that is, when compared with their modern counterparts ; yet the ammunition manufacturers must keep the necessary machinery ready since they never know when they may be called upon for a consign-

14

ment of some of this old ammunition. Their overhead expenses are thereby kept at a higher figure than is really necessary, and this means that ammunition costs more than it need ; because if the manufacturers were to know that they would only be called upon for modern ammunition, they would be enabled to convert all their machinery and not have it lying idle for long periods, and this in turn would mean that our cartridges would cost us less.

The fault, and its remedy, lies with gunsmiths. Not very long ago I saw a beautiful best-quality double rifle which a young tyro had allowed his gunsmith to persuade him to have built for the old ·375-bore cartridge—or if it was that in his ignorance he ordered a ·375 himself, then his gunsmith was greatly to blame for not pointing out the mistake ; since it would have cost not one penny more to have chambered and·regulated the rifle for the modern ·375 magnum cartridge, when the sportsman would have been vastly better pleased with his rifle and able to do things with it which he could not dream of doing with the weapon as built. Possibly the fault originated with somebody who wrote a book describing his experiences big game hunting all over the world with a ·375 magnum, and who was too lazy to write the word " magnum " each time he had occasion to refer to his rifle. If rifles were no longer built for obsolete cartridges, there would be no fear of such mistakes occurring : the designation ·375, alone, would be sufficient.

There is no earthly necessity for all the cartridges that are on the market at the present time. All that is necessary is to choose the best in each group, and for gunsmiths to agree to only build rifles of those particular calibres, chambered and regulated only for those cartridges. If everybody could build double rifles for rimless cartridges as reliable as Westley Richards, then rimless cartridges would be all that would be required ; but since that is a patent of this firm which they probably wish to keep for themselves, then let us choose one flanged and one rimless cartridge in each group so that all tastes are catered for : those who prefer doubles and those who, for any reason, prefer magazines, and see to what extent we can whittle down the list from its present 120-odd calibres.

Starting at the bottom of the list, since the ·240 is already obtainable in both flanged and rimless form it should be retained in preference to either the ·242 or ·246 which are only obtainable as rimless and flanged respectively, whilst its ballistics and trajectory are unsurpassed in this group. This caters for the sportsman who likes a very light rifle for deer stalking and similar sport. There is no real necessity then for anything between this and ·300. Of the ·300's, for the man who wants to shoot the lighter varieties of soft-skinned game and who does not expect to be tackling dangerous animals, the ·375/·300 (" Super-Thirty ") is there both in flanged and rimless form with ballistics equally as good as those of the modern edition of the Springfield ·300 withal at a lower chamber pressure. Three different weights of bullet are available.

Of the medium bores, the ·375 magnum stands alone and is the obvious one to be retained. Since, however, the ·318 has such an immense following in all parts of the world, he would need to be a very brave man who would dare to suggest its elimination from the list ! So, although it is not really necessary, let it by all means be kept alive.

For the man who does a fair amount of work amongst heavy and dangerous game and does not feel that he would have genuine confidence in a bullet of less than 400 grains, there is the ·400 which has long proved itself ; with the ·404 as its magazine edition.

When we get to rifles primarily intended for use against heavy and dangerous game, it is perfectly ridiculous to keep the eleven flanged cartridges at present on the market. It is true that the ·450's and ·500's are only built to order nowadays ; but it would be much better if they were not even built to that extent. Of the various cartridges in the ·470 group, the ·465 and ·470 are the best if for no other reason because they have a lower chamber pressure than the others. Of these two, when expanding bullets are used I do not think that there is anything to choose between them ; but when solids are used on elephants and rhino, but particularly elephant, I am not so sure. I have shot about 100 elephant with a 26-inch-barrelled ·470, and was a trifle surprised and disappointed to find that on several occasions I had to give a beast a second shot which I was, and am, certain would not have been necessary had I been using the ·465 or ·450 No 2. I put it down to the fact that the bullet thrown by the ·470 tapers considerably more towards the nose than I care about when solids are being used. In my experience a solid bullet should be absolutely parallel with a round nose if it is to be relied upon to retain a straight course always after entering any part of an elephant. The bullet thrown by the ·465 is of much better shape than that of the ·470—in fact, it is just about ideal. I do not think that my disappointment with the ·470 was merely coincidence : I have shot about double the number of elephant with the ·465, and round about three times the number with the ·450 No. 2 ; so that I have had many opportunities of comparing the performance of the different cartridges. I must admit, however, that I did not trace the course of those shots fired from the ·470 which seemed to necessitate second shots ; since it takes some little time to dissect an elephant's head and find out what has happened to a bullet, and candour compels me to admit that a great many of my elephant were poached, which all too frequently means a rapid retreat from the scene of operations just as soon as ever the ivory has been chopped out ! I am, however, firmly convinced that the bullet thrown by the ·465 is of better shape than the ·470, and accordingly ought to be retained in preference.

For the magazine enthusiast, there is the ·416 which has a lower chamber pressure than the ·425.

As far as genuine elephant rifles are concerned, since the professional hunter may occasionally need something more powerful than the ·465, I should be inclined to recommend the ·577 in preference to the ·600 since it has all the power that could ever be needed, and can be built appreciably lighter. For the magazine man, there is the ·505 which is to be preferred to the rimless ·500, because the ammunition for the latter is not loaded in England.

So that there, instead of some 120-odd cartridges we can manage perfectly satisfactorily with a dozen—a " baker's dozen " if the ·318 is to be included.

Large-Bores.	Large-Medium Bores.	Medium-Bores.	Small-Bores.
·577	·416	·375 magnum	·375/·300
·505	·404	·318 (?)	·240
·465	·400		

CASES

A good rifle surely deserves a good case. Even if you seldom use it other than when travelling, just think how your fine rifles may, and certainly will, be knocked about when jolting about in a lorry. The leather-covered oak case with brass corners is out and away the best type and is well worth the extra money ; it will last indefinitely and outlive several of the ordinary canvas-covered cases. You can always buy cases second-hand at considerably reduced prices ; but if you are buying two double-barrelled weapons, or a double and a magazine with a detachable stock, you can have just one double case built to accommodate both weapons, and will find it considerably cheaper than getting two cases.

LOADING REVOLVERS

If you decide to add a revolver to your equipment, either to keep beside your pillow at night or to carry with you always, *never load more than five chambers*. Let the hammer down on the empty chamber, and the weapon is as harmless as a pipe : you can throw it about to your heart's content without the slightest risk of it " going off " and shooting either you or your servants.   This custom of only loading five chambers originated in America in the days of the old single-action " Frontier " Colt.   The single-action revolver did not have a rebounding hammer ; accordingly, if all six chambers were loaded, the striker of the hammer actually rested on the cap of the cartridge. This meant that the slightest blow on the hammer would discharge the gun.   The modern double-action revolver has a rebounding hammer which is supposed to render it safe from accidental discharge ; but only the very trusting would rely upon this supposition.

A brother-in-law of mine, when in uniform one day and with a service revolver in a holster at his waist, for some reason best known to himself decided to crank the engine of a car instead of letting the driver do it.   As he swung the motor, his revolver, loaded in all six chambers, fell out of its holster and struck either the ground or one of the dumb-irons of the car—the point is immaterial ; it " went off " and shot him through the upper part of the left arm, fortunately without doing any serious harm. But if you picture the position of a man cranking a car and having a revolver drop out of a holster on his belt (" Sam Browne "), you will realize that it was only a matter of inches and that bullet would have blown his brains out.   Beyond the fact that it was a service revolver of the era of the ·455, I know nothing about the gun : it was probably a Webley ; but might just as easily have been either a Smith & Wesson or a Colt.   The fact remains that it was a modern double-action weapon and was accidentally discharged through being dropped.

No outdoor man, accustomed to having a loaded revolver always within reach of his hand, ever loads more than five chambers.   As we look at it, if you cannot extricate yourself from a tight corner with five shots from a heavy revolver, you will not succeed in doing so with six. For the simple reason that if you haven't managed to shoot him with five chances, the other fellow will certainly have shot you before ever you come to that empty chamber. In the same way, if it is a lion that has got hold of you at night, if you cannot persuade him to drop you with five shots, you will not have the hope of that proverbial snowball in the nether regions of doing so with six. Accordingly, why take the risk of shooting yourself (which wouldn't matter in the least) or one of your servants (which would matter a great deal), when there is absolutely nothing to be gained by it ?

Never load more than five chambers of your revolver ; and let the hammer down on the empty chamber.